Captain Radford's Diary

Published

in

A Limited Edition of 500 copies

Copy No.

———————

Grant Books
Victoria Square, Droitwich
Worcestershire WR9 8DE

Captain Radford's Diary

George Radford

Grant Books, Worcestershire
1992

ISBN 0 907 186 19X

Typeset in Baskerville
and printed by
Severnside Printers Limited

Published in an edition of 500 copies
by
Grant Books
Victoria Square, Droitwich,
Worcestershire
WR9 8DE

Contents

Foreword

George Radford had an adventurous life, both afloat and ashore. He went to sea as an apprentice with the British Tanker Company in 1929, when the British Merchant Navy was still the largest in the world, and rose through the ranks to chief officer. As an RNR officer he served throughout World War II in naval vessels and at the end of the conflict he returned to the Merchant Navy, sailing as master of one of the earliest roll-on-roll-off ferries before joining the Trinity House pilotage service.

His active retirement after many years as a pilot included an adventurous episode as security officer at a West African diamond mine, running a chandlery in Australia and, briefly, a return to pilotage in New Zealand, where he finally settled.

I did not meet Captain Thomas George Radford until he became a founder member, and later a fellow, of the London-based Nautical Institute, an independent international professional body for promoting high standards at sea. I was editing the Institute's journal *Seaways*, where George's strongly-held views on maritime matters were often to be found in the letters column. Always full of good seamanlike sense, his comments ranged widely, from passenger liners to (not surprisingly) the proper briefing of the pilot on boarding a vessel. His last letter dealt with anchoring, and then, sadly, *Seaways* in 1989 carried the news of his death in Auckland, New Zealand, at the age of 76.

It is a pleasure to commend George's "Diary". Firstly it is a 'good read', a rattling yarn in a respectable sea story tradition. But it is more than that: it is a personal record of a way of life that has vanished as completely as that of the cargo-carrying square-riggers of the 19th century. When George Radford went to sea, the British merchant flag, the Red Ensign, flew from the sterns of over 8,000 ships; now there are fewer than 500. The British seafarer is an endangered species.

The ships in which he served his apprenticeship had crews of around 50; today vessels three times their size may have only half-a-dozen on board. At the same time equipment on board has moved from the fairly primitive to the computerised hi-tech. It is good that he recorded his experiences before they are forgotten.

David G. Sanders.

1. Going to Sea

Taking to the sea was no family tradition or even a youthful urge for adventure – it was a foregone conclusion resulting from my mother's two Cunard crossings of the Atlantic as a young woman. From family stories it seems she was deeply impressed with the life of the ship's officers and, as I approached my sixteenth year, she took great pains to keep me well informed of the difficulties attached to obtaining an apprenticeship with a reputable shipping company, especially at the advent of depression times. Some years later after she died I came across an old diary which confirmed the family theory. It seems I was destined for the sea as she floated in romantic youthfulness among passengers and officers during her crossings to and from the United States of America.

I remember little of the day of departure from home except for not wanting my family to accompany me to the station. My best pal, the boy next door, helped me with my trunk and as we stood on the platform waiting for the train he pointed to a spelling mistake on the destination label – it was an example of how bedevilled I was to remain from the effects of an incomplete education. Looking back, it would seem I was blessed with an extra dose of common sense, will and diligence, which made up for other shortcomings. My family were business people and the intellectual side of life was never too prominent – even

Off to sea, 8th August 1929

the facts and pitfalls of life were carefully avoided. Before leaving home my mother told me that my father would have a word with me before I left – I remember the words quite well: "Well, Son, I suppose your mother has told you everything. Don't forget to look after your feet, you know the trouble I have with mine. Always cut your toe-nails square and your finger-nails round".

After spending the night with friends in Southampton I presented myself early the next morning at the office of the shipping agents in Canute Road (how can I forget it), where I was introduced

1

to a strapping fellow one year older than myself called Yeates. He had sailed for a year as deck boy in one of Holder Bros. ships and was to be my shipmate; although a very fine fellow it was obvious I was going to be the under-dog. Things then moved pretty quickly and we were soon in the agents' launch speeding down the Southampton Water and climbing the steep accommodation ladder of my first ship, the ss *British Progress,* an oil tanker of some 10,000 tons deadweight. It was owned by the British Tanker Company Limited of London, which was a subsidiary of the Anglo Persian Oil Company Ltd. So, at about 9.30am on the 9th August 1929 and within minutes of lugging our gear safely on board, the task of getting under way was in progress.

British Progress *in heavy weather*

Recollections of my first few days at sea have always been hazy, I remember the two buckets I became attached to– one for my vomit, the other cleaning water. My sea-sickness was pretty miserable, and it must have been well down the Portuguese coast before I started to take real notice of what was going on around me.

And so life at sea for me began and like all young people I quickly picked up the dialogue and ways of the people round about me. Although in our home I was accustomed to regular chores, the strict routine aboard ship was quite a different matter – with emphasis on a full day's work on deck, a prescribed course of studies and the three meals each day taken in the dining saloon, for which a change into uniform after cleaning ourselves was a prerequisite. Fresh water was never plentiful. Every ton of water carried was one ton less of cargo freight earnings. A bath took the form of a bucket of warm water carried from the galley or pantry and placed in the bath – a stand-up job. The same facilities were used for washing our clothes, with dire penalties for making a mess (anybody can clean, we were told repeatedly, you must learn to KEEP it clean).

The day of arrival was always an exciting time, more so if it were a port which we had never visited before; part of building the travelled image of course, although the underlying reason was the anticipation

On board the British Progress *in 1931 when I was eighteen – second from the left and holding a white sun-helmet. Frank Mann my fellow apprentice is beside me wearing his khaki topee. We were part of the gang of seamen engaged cleaning the cargo tanks – a filthy job which could sometimes be dangerous.*

of letters from home. There was nothing more important in my life than receiving my mail, and I believe that was the feeling of all people who spent most of their time at sea. (During the time about which I write, a good shipping company would expect their officers to serve continuously for at least one year before applying for leave. The normal length of time was two years, by which time one could expect a spell at home of two months on pay.) As time went on our work routine was broken with periods of watch-keeping. We liked this, as it gave us an opportunity to browse in the chart-room and taste the rudiments of navigation. The corner of the bridge-wing in the darkness was also a convenient place to recite the 'Articles' (the details of the nautical rule of the road, which had to be learnt by heart), or think of home.

One passage succeeded another to places in most parts of the world, usually all radiating from the Persian Gulf – we must have been very fit to cope with the extremes of such places as Svolvaer north of the Arctic Circle. The policy of transferring apprentices to different vessels in the fleet was considered necessary in order to gain experience with the cargoes and ships themselves, and so as my time in the *Progress* became longer and longer, my slight apprehension grew. The periodic appointments among the officers and engineers, with occasional changes of crew became a blurred sea of faces, some listened to and learnt from, some admired or envied, whilst a few stood out as permanent marks in my life. Among these indelible characters was Captain Ralph Thoburn, disliked by most for his strict discipline, but in my opinion a man of great courage and with whom I was later to sail as his junior officer. There was a Mr Jones, our third mate from North Wales. He was middle aged, tall and cadaverous; unkindly described by some as something of a cap-badge-collector. He was without doubt a very thorough seaman, claiming my awe and admiration in spite of the tobacco juice he squirted around to our disgust. He taught us to sew canvas properly, rope awnings and other skills not found in our text books. After the evening meal in the dining saloon he would often enthral us with stories of his days in sailing ships. As a young boy he first went to sea in the famous schooners which sailed from places

Sewing canvas while serving on the British Progress

like Port Madog to fish the cod off the Newfoundland Banks. They were small vessels with their holds filled with salt. His graphic stories of salting down the cod were often interspersed with odious comparisons to our conditions of going to sea. (More than once he told me I would never make a seaman as long as I had a hole in my arse.)

Then there was a Mr. Wilson, a real character who was a tubby, jovial, snuff addict and whose nose and upper lip were permanently stained. His periodic sneezes could be heard all over the ship. He gave great help and encouragement to us with our studies. He taught us the principle and adjustments of the sextant. Mr. Wilson was the second officer and as such prided himself on his navigation. He seemed to specialize in the special rules and quick methods – many of which I carried in my head all the time I was at sea, such as:

1.5 /Height of Eye = Distance of Horizon
or: Sec. Latitude + Sine Declination = Sine True Amplitude

Another who stands out in my mind is Ronald Friendship. We were third-year apprentices together in the *British Commodore*. Small of stature, Friendship lived up to his name with a very big heart and we were the very best of shipmates and friends. (As I hope to recount later, we both aspired to our respective dreamed-of zeniths.) Although constantly together we were never at odds with each other; he called me Taffy and pulled my leg about my Welsh accent. Our cabin was aft in the poop-space in the same alleyway as the refrigerator and engine-room access, where the incessant main engine clatter was punctured from time to time by thuds and bangs from chunks of meat flung out of the refrigerator.

Ronnie and I were both in our nineteenth year and our needs were increasing, so to earn some extra money we undertook to wash officers' clothes. Ten shillings a month was the charge, which was only five bob each. It could not have given us much more than an extra pound a month, but a pound note was worth something in those days – we could buy from the captain (through the steward) half a pound of Capstan fine cut tobacco for four shillings, which with care we would make last for four weeks. Looking back, I think they were the happiest days of my life, and although memories dim with time, some will always be remembered. It was always hot in our cabin, especially east of Suez, when a pair of briefs would be our normal attire during watch-below periods. There we would be busy studying, ironing clothes, writing letters or sleeping. Sleep was our greatest desire – or maybe it was food. There was little to choose between them. If I had the evening watch Ronnie would ask me to wake him at midnight when I went below so that he could revel in the delight of rolling a cigarette and going to sleep again. We were never allowed to keep the

Ronnie and myself, he with his cap askew as we do our dhobi, probably a Saturday afternoon on the poop deck

middle watch, so our next would be the morning watch; in this way each apprentice would have eight hours sleep. Even in those days Ronnie had the makings of a barrel chest, so with my Land of Song background our duets almost equalled in volume the main-engine. (Years later we stood together in St.Michael's Church, Cornhill, for the annual service of the Honourable Company of Master Mariners, and as our shoulders touched we resoundingly sang our old favourite hymn 'Cwm Rhondda.')

Returning to the narrative and the unusually long period I was spending aboard the *British Progress,* the inevitable finally happened when one night steaming up the Red Sea a wireless message was received ordering my transfer to another of the company's ships. It came at an unusual time to say the least. Captain Thoburn had requested a portrait photograph of himself to send home and had offered me a shilling to get it developed and printed before reaching Suez. It was a hot and sticky evening as my mate and I struggled to keep the water cool enough for the hypo to do its work in the darkened cabin, when suddenly the door opened flooding the room with alleyway light. "Is it nearly ready" said the Old Man. They were a poor set of prints that came out of the 'fixer', and the captain complained of their quality so I said to him.... "what do you expect for a bob"!

After the deathly hush I was sent up to the monkey island for the remainder of the night, where in the darkness my mind ranged over the dire consequences for such disrespect. It was whilst suffering this mental anguish that 'Sparks' must have received the coded message concerning my transfer on arrival at Port Suez.

In hindsight I think the three years spent in the *'Progress'* was too long – I had become a bit too cocksure of myself.

The Old Man sent for me when he received the message and told me to go below and get some sleep in preparation for packing my gear the next morning. As I made to leave his cabin he advised me to get some tobacco from the chief steward because he did not think it was available on board my next ship. We dropped anchor in Suez Bay fairly close to my new ship, the ss *British Empress,* and Captain Thoburn sent for me to say good-bye with some words of advice never to be forgotten: "Assert yourself always – but don't be arrogant". I was very soon to learn how thoughtful the captain had been when the first thing I discovered on reaching the *'Empress'* was that she had been out of bonded stores for weeks.

The *British Empress* was an older vessel with a slightly raked single case funnel and shrouds with ratlines. Her steering quadrant was sited above the poop deck with the chains leading forward to a small engine house. Although an oil burning ship, she constantly belched black oily smoke from her funnel. A fair wind was the apprentices nightmare of trying to keep the white paintwork around the amidships clean. Another horrible job was cleaning the whistle on the funnel because, unlike the more modern ships, there was no fixed steel ladder, only a permanently rigged gantline for hoisting the junior apprentice in a bosun's chair. If the chap was wise he would wrap sacking around his knees for protection against the heat of the funnel. I used to think the only good thing about being in the 'Empress' was the fact that I was the senior boy and the more unpleasant tasks could be put on to the other chap. In retrospect I suppose she was good for some one-upmanship when on the subject of your last ship (the 'Empress' for example had unusual compass deviations, which were considered due to her octagonal steel wheelhouse).

After a few months we had a cargo for the U.K. and I was granted my first proper leave. During this time my family had moved and the holiday seemed very strange to me. Most of the time my relatives wanted to see me in my uniform and the sort of questions they asked about my life at sea I used to consider rather silly. An aunt once asked me what happened to the ship at night. Looking perplexed, I replied nothing. She then asked how can you see where you are going – it was so obvious that there was no salt water running in my family. By this time I had become interested in girls, and with one right next door my knowledge and understanding of the female sex received considerable impetus! It also became evident that I was inclined to be shy, a little backward about going forward as the saying goes, at least as far as the fair sex was concerned. I overcame this gaucheness, after becoming more accustomed to female society. (It would be fair to say that for many like myself, tied to the tanker life with its constant and gruelling demands over such long periods – often years – it deprived some people of a basic aspect of the business of living, sometimes with irreparable harm in later life.)

All too soon the letter instructing me to join my next ship came, and with it the end of the fussing, over-feeding and par-

My mother, early in the morning as I left home after my memorable first leave

ticular happiness for my mother who had waited so long for my homecoming. I am not ashamed to say my affection for my mother was tremendous. (Even after marriage we still wrote to each other frequently.)

Joining the ss *British Commodore* and meeting Ron Friendship, my new fellow apprentice, soon took all thoughts of home from my mind, and it became the most happy ship for me – ending all too soon whilst as a fourth year boy I was transferred yet again. The company was certainly making up for lost time. Leaving the '*Commodore*' was a sad parting; compensated however by my next and final ship which was 'brand new'.

To me the mv *British Splendour* was the last word – one of the latest class and fitted with the up-to-date equipment of the time. The apprentices' large cabin was situated in the spacious section of the amidships and she was capable of a full twelve knots. Captain Joseph Storey Commander, the master, was a well known character of whom stories were prevalent around the fleet. He was that kind of ship-master one could never forget, setting a high standard and expecting a high standard from his officers. A further pleasant surprise was the chief officer, under whom I served when in the *British Progress*. Alec Baillie was an outstanding officer who earned the respect of most who sailed with him – he had the rare quality at sea of a high sense of humour. He went on to command and eventually become one of the marine superintendents.

As soon as I joined the ship the captain took me in hand in preparation for the forthcoming examination for the second mate's certificate. Apparently I was his first cadet who was likely to finish the term of apprenticeship actually at sea and under his command. It seems he had strong views concerning the company rules which stated that in the event of an apprentice completing his 'time' at sea, he was to be placed on the ship's articles as able seaman and paid accordingly. Captain Commander considered it was unfair to train a young man for four years to become an officer and then sign him on the register as an A.B. He decided that should the situation ever arise with him he would sign the young man on as fourth mate, and pay the difference out of his own pocket.

Commander was a man of many talents, among them being his skill at french polishing. He was able to hold his respect as master and at the same time devote his spare time to removing the dockyard 'finish' on such things as saloon fittings and replacing it with a smooth glossy appearance associated with quality hardwood chairs and tables.

Few were excluded from his enthusiasm so naturally his primary assisting pupils were the apprentices. It was a knack of course but in time we picked it up. Although using the shellac left its mark on our fingers, the results were considered well worth our efforts. The chief officer however had different views on how our hours of deck-work should be spent, and thought it was taking things too far when Commander decided to unscrew the two wooden seats from the crew's toilets, bring them amidships and set about french polishing them. He excelled himself on these items of bare wood – so much so that on one Sunday morning 'rounds' the bosun remarked they were too good for sailor's hairy backsides and would be more suitable as picture frames for the King and Queen hung in the crew's quarters.

Previous to this time, completion of my apprenticeship could not have come soon enough, but as the year 1933 progressed I became less and less happy about the completion of my four years – there were so many ships laid up with a very large number of certificated officers on the dole. Captain Commander was well aware of my anxiety and even offered to give me as a gift one of his two sextants should I be successful in passing first time the second mate's examination. Well, it so happened my time expired as we made our way through the Mediterranean with a cargo for the U.K. Purfleet was the terminal for discharge and Tilbury for signing off the crew. True to his word I had been entered on the register as fourth mate and duly given a discharge book with this entry – I felt very proud. Commander had paid the half-crown for the discharge book and also made my pay up as promised. He also firmly reminded me of his offer regarding the sextant. Returning to the ship the chief officer asked me to stay on board a further two days for the completion of painting the amidship section, which had been interrupted by bad weather in the English Channel – this was in preparation for an inspection by one of the London marine superintendents. Finally I was leaving the ship with people's good wishes and the free railway warrant to which Captain Commander thought I was entitled.

2. The First Appointment

Although it was wonderful to be home again, my future career with the existing economics of the time weighed heavily on my mind. The nearest nautical college was in Cardiff, which meant meant fees, lodgings and text books. The General Strike of 1926 followed by the Depression, from which many business people like my family never properly recovered, made it necessary that I should start earning some money as a prerequisite to anything. Jobs among the crews of the Cardiff and Swansea tramp steamers were hard to get – so many of them were laid up. I tried writing to my own company for a job in the fo'c'sle and they replied there was a waiting list of certificated officers for the jobs on deck, and that they would be pleased to hear from me when I was successful in passing my examination. A short while before writing that letter, after I had been home for about a bare week, I had received a letter from Britannic House in London saying they noted I had been issued with a free railway warrant from Purfleet to Swansea. They requested the amount (something between a pound and thirty shillings) be refunded, pointing out it had been issued in error, also that had I purchased a ticket at the railway station myself it would have cost that much more (about a few shillings). We were nonplussed but had to comply. There was no doubt that for people like myself the early thirties were bad times.

So for several weeks I tramped the docks of Swansea. Some advised me to try other ports, but at least it was my home port which saved me the expense of travel and lodgings, so I persevered. The day came when after bribing a bosun with pints of beer, I was given a promise that he would point me out to the chief officer of his ship on the following day during the process of picking the crew outside the Shipping Office. He kept his word, and thrusting my vellum indentures into the mate's hand for scrutiny was given the nod and thus found myself on the inside of the double doors signing on the articles of the ss *Matina* as quartermaster. This entitled me to an extra ten shillings a month over A.B.'s money. We were ordered aboard at midnight to sail with the morning tide – bound for Kingston, Jamaica.

The *Matina* was owned by Elders & Fyffes and of course was solely engaged at that period transporting bananas from the West Indies to the U.K. After the four years in oil tankers she seemed like a large yacht to me with her white hull and buff funnel and steaming at fourteen knots. There were twelve passengers and apart from our tricks at the wheel the quartermaster's duties were confined to the boat deck and the comforts of the passengers. I found the changed life rather pleasant and all too soon we arrived at Kingston and started to load the cargo. This was soon interrupted, however, when the area was struck by a hurricane, causing severe damage to plantations and supply routes. But it is an ill wind that brings nobody any good, because we enjoyed the unplanned visit to off-shore anchorages around the island where it was possible to load the bananas from barges. For myself it meant more days, more dollars (a welcome bonus). The sight of Montego Bay as we lay at anchor in the lagoon was of such beauty that it has remained imprinted in my mind to this day. The low key sing-song chant of the Jamaicans (male and female) as they smoothly mounted the gangways each with a stem of bananas carried on the head in single file procession, was a fascinating experience. Finally the banana bins in the holds were full and we sailed away on our northern North Atlantic crossing for home.

The prospects of a second trip were dim, but Christmas was not too far off and my eagerness to enjoy the first festive season since the age of fifteen was great. The *Matina* paid off in Avonmouth where the cargo was to be discharged, and although it was getting dark by the time we finally secured alongside the quay, it did not stop the shore and Shipping Office people pouring aboard for the business of paying off on board. A night's sleep with a meal under our belts would have been appreciated by the Swansea crew before making the journey back to South Wales, but there was little philanthropy displayed by shipowners. I believe it was the first time I had ever seen a five-pound note. Certainly they were the first I had ever handled when picking up two of them plus three one-pound notes and some silver from the table along with my 'paper' discharge. At the monthly rate of pay of eight pounds twelve shillings and sixpence my pay off made me feel rich and I couldn't get home fast enough with my wealth – with a regulation free railway warrant this time!

On the 28th November 1933 I reached Cardiff to commence attendance at the Nautical Branch of the Cardiff Technical College in preparation for the second mate's certificate. After essential expenditure on text books and school fees, my total funds amounted to eleven pounds which was placed in the Post Office Savings Bank. This together with the unemployment benefit of fourteen shillings per week I hoped to make last long enough to complete the course and sit the examination. Thanks to the British Tanker Company's training scheme we had a fairly good basic knowledge of the syllabus set by the Board of Trade examiners, but of course there was a great deal more to learn, not least being the idiosyncrasies and pet questions of the local examiner. So I studied every night in my digs, only allowing myself a cinema seat and bag of chips on the Saturday night. Lady Luck must have been on my shoulder and I passed the exam. (A particular friend of mine whom I considered more advanced than myself failed in the dreaded seamanship room where all the questions and answers were oral. Quite by chance I met him two years later to discover he was sailing as A.B. in a tramp steamer.)

My small supply of money had been stretched to the limit, so with my return-half bus ticket I returned home to Swansea. I withdrew the last ten shillings from the Post Office on 26th February 1934, leaving a credit balance of fourpence. The first thing was to inform the B.T.C. that I had a second mate's certificate and was awaiting their instructions, to which the reply was as expected. 'Congratulations, we will put your name on our waiting list'.

There was the gnawing worry about the lack of funds for the purchase of a secondhand sextant and some suitable officer's gear, and as the weeks went by the temptation to seek a job in the fo'c'sle of some ship became very great. Eventually the letter arrived. I was to join the ss. *British Lord* as third officer at Plymouth on 29th March 1934. How my family managed to help me to fit myself out I will never know, but I duly presented myself at the Shipping Office via the agents. After producing my brand new second mate's certificate, I was introduced to the master of the *British Lord*, a gentleman called Cunningham, who from that day until the 14th January 1935 which was the day I left, seemed to concentrate on making my life rather unpleasant. I used to attribute this situation to my very ancient sextant (it was cut to fifteen seconds) and according to Cunningham was unreliable. This may have accounted for his lack of confidence in me, although the chief officer was more sympathetic and considered the real reason was due to the bad stomach he suffered as a result of being a prisoner of war in Germany.

I did my job to the best of my ability for nearly a year, when I applied for a transfer and was very happy to join the ss *British General* – with no other in command than the Captain Thoburn. We had something in common from my first ship, the *'Progress'*. Life as an officer took on a different aspect and with his encouragement and firm efficiency I soon regained my self confidence.

The *British General* continued to trade to the Persian Gulf, loading cargoes of oil, mostly for terminals in the Mediterranean, until the spring of 1936, by which time the necessary sea time had been served for me to consider the next examination for the first mates certificate. Being gainfully employed not only took care of my savings, but also enabled me to refund my parents. There was no doubt things were beginning to take shape for me. Thoughts of survival receded and gave way to plans and ambitions for the future, such as the Royal Naval Reserve, Trinity House Pilotage and even a complete change to passenger and cargo vessels. Charles H. Brown and his *Nicholls's Concise Guide, Seamanship & Nautical Knowledge, Meteorology For Masters & Mates* had no opportunity to collect dust on my book shelf. But I was plagued with thought of those who had the head-start on me with education.

3. Pre-War

After taking my leave of the *British General,* I lost no time in establishing myself back at the Cardiff Technical College where, unlike the previous occasion, I was able to pursue the curriculum at a more leisurely pace, passing the examination at the first attempt.

With my first mate's certificate firmly in my pocket I turned my attention to joining the Royal Naval Reserve, but first a personal visit had to be made to the head office in London. It was my seventh year of service with the British Tanker Company and the closest I had been to the fountain head was a cursory acknowledgement from a visiting marine superintendent. It must be said however that the staff afloat had been informed that visits to the London office would be welcomed when people happened to be in the vicinity on leave. Britannic House in Finsbury Circus was all a large shipping establishment should be, to my mind, so after a respectable wait I was first seen by no other a person than Captain Baillie, with whom I had sailed on the two previous occasions. He had become an assistant marine superintendent. After a few words of encouragement he ushered me into the presence of the chief marine superintendent. Respect, bordering on fear of our superiors in those days, reduced me to a trembling state of inadequacy. I clearly remember this fearful man consulting what looked like my file which lay open on his large desk, and mentioning the *British Lord,* my first ship as an officer, saying "of course we do not always take too much notice of some master's confidential reports". Then as a prelude to my dismissal he asked if I had any special reason for making the visit, and like a fool I asked what the prospects were for my promotion! I cannot remember his reply, but with the ink hardly dry on my first mates 'ticket' I imagine it was full of pith.

With the bit between my teeth I hastened away from Britannic House with some words of warning and went looking for St. James's Park, where at Queen Anne's Mansions was the office of the Admiral Commanding Reserves. Time has dimmed the details concerning these initial steps as far as the Naval Reserve was concerned – somehow or other I acquired a book on the 'Rules and Regulations of the Royal Naval Reserve' and set about making personal contact with established RNR officers. This was not an easy task because the head office at that time did not encourage their officers to become RNR men; they were afraid of losing too many in the event of mobilization. It did not deter me, however, because somehow or other I felt the ultimate goal did not include oil tankers, and in any case I had already applied to the Union-Castle Line for a position in their fleet. Entry into good and well established shipping companies was not easy and the pre-sea training of *Conway* or *Worcester*, plus a permanent commission in the Reserve, almost a prerequisite.

This exciting time of my life was interrupted when a recall came to join the *ss British Officer* at my home port of Swansea as third mate on 29th July 1936. But this time it was with a different feeling that I unpacked my trunk in the cabin and carefully stacked my collection of text books on the shelves – firmly secured against bad weather – I had been accepted by the office of the Admiral Commanding Reserve as a **Probationary Acting Sub-Lieutenant, R.N.R.**

The only outstanding thing in my memory concerning the *British Officer* was the master, Captain Watkin Watkin-Thomas, a rare character, whose Welsh accent and unpredictable ways can never be forgotten. The story goes he commanded an auxiliary schooner acting as a Q-Ship during the First World War. He chain-smoked his cigarettes with the aid of a piece of twisted wire, having a loop each end – one for the cigarette, the other slipped over his finger. He was never known to visit the bridge unless his presence was really needed, nevertheless he insisted upon being kept informed by voice-pipe. He was much over-weight and drank his gin from a small wine glass; entertaining only when there were passengers aboard. He seemed to like some company during the first watch. The engineer officers had little cause to be fond of Watkin-Thomas due to his intense displeasure whenever thick smoke was emitted from the funnel. His written standing orders were that if after informing the engineer on watch the smoke persisted, the chief engineer was to be informed immediately. On one such occasion eastbound through the Straits of Gibraltar with the usual following wind, black smoke suddenly started to pour out of the funnel, enveloping the bridge and forming an arc of poor visibility right ahead. After informing the engine room I sent a message to the chief engineer – but it still belched thickly so I informed the master, who, disturbed from his evening relaxation, climbed slowly to the bridge and ordered the engines stopped. He then gave orders to hoist the two red lights, which showed that the ship was not under command, and instructed me to make an entry in the log that the ship was unable to proceed due to impaired visibility caused by thick black smoke!

As I recall the *British Officer* was a fairly unhappy ship, which often occurs when there happens to be a much talked about prominent person providing the subject matter. It was therefore with no great feeling of regret that on arriving at Abadan for yet another cargo I received instructions to transfer to the ss *British Duchess*, already berthed a few jetties away.

And so on 13th April 1937 I joined the *'Duchess'* as third mate and commenced my first experience with an Indian crew, the ship being referred to as being on the coast, meaning she was employed mostly around the Indian Ocean and Red Sea ports.

Changing crews in Bombay

For nearly two years I served in this ship. It was a very happy time for me. The second mate, Ronald Marsh, and I became great friends and were to remain so for many years. Being the junior officer I had a great deal to learn and Marsh was just the meticulous officer to impart his skill and know-how. All the charts he kept scrupulously up to date and I studied intently his systems used for his various duties as navigating officer with the object of emulating his methods.

Of the crew, I found the Goanese stewards a bit strange at first but soon discovered them to be thoroughly clean and reliable. There was no chief steward; instead a butler assumed the duties supervising the catering staff and issuing of provisions. The books dealing with these stores, however, were the responsibility of the third officer, for the keeping of which I was paid an extra pound a month. Actually it was quite a task on top of my other duties, but those were the days when hard work was the price one paid for gainful employment. As our superiors were quick to say, the more you know about the

consumption of stores the better equipped you are to detect irregu-
larities when reaching command.

Our eastern routine was interrupted with a cargo for Europe
which suited Ronnie Marsh well, because this time he had sufficient
time served to enable him to sit the Master's Certificate examination.
So during August 1937, whilst undergoing periodic docking at Sunderland, we said goodbye to each other. (We did not see each other
again until the closing stages of the war when by a chance meeting in
one of the streets of Port Elizabeth we came face to face. One could
never forget his wide grin. He was wearing his RAF stripes and I was
a Lieutenant-Commander RNR. We had a lot of past ground to catch
up on.)

Apart from holding our jobs during these very competitive
times, the thoughts most uppermost in our minds were of promotion,
to be able to start putting in to practice the things we were busy
learning as juniors. Mine came just before the *British Duchess* was ready
to sail from her docking at Sunderland. It was the usual letter from the
head office hoping I would continue to merit the confidence they
placed in me together with my new rate of pay as second officer.

So it was that on 16th August 1937 with my two new stripes and
in my twenty-fourth year we sailed for the Persian Gulf. I was very
conscious of my new responsibilities in connection with the navigation and the keeping of the middle watch – that time when most of the
ship's company would be asleep, even the captain when his presence
on the bridge was not essential. Captain Goodchild was our master, a
mild mannered man with whom it was a pleasure to serve under (like
so many others he joined the list of people I was to come in contact
with in the years that followed). Together with my step up to second
mate came two extra new jobs. One was the taking charge of the
mooring and unmooring operations at the after end of the ship, the
other being the officer in charge of the regular lifeboat drills –
starboard side boats only being my responsibility. Both these tasks
brought me in closer contact with the Indian crew and an essential
part of the efficiency of these operations was learning to speak some
of their language – I found a good way to practise was with the stand-
by quartermaster during a quiet watch.

Abadan to Aden was the most frequent voyage, taking eight or
nine days, depending on the time of the year in relation to the
monsoons. It took thirty-six hours to discharge the cargo of fuel oil
and another week to get back to the Shatt al Arab, the river on which
Abadan stands.

Captain Radford's Diary

The south-west monsoon played a big part in our life as far as normal duties were concerned; from April to October the south-west winds would blow very strongly causing the steep sea to be constantly keeping the main deck under water. With much rain and heavy cloud navigation became difficult. I speak of course before the advent of Decca Navigator chains, satellite navigation or, even the gyro compass as far as our ships were concerned. I recall so clearly the times we strove to catch a glimpse of the sun through the scudding clouds coming up close to the noon position with albeit a doubtful horizon. Even during the near perfect weather of the north-east monsoon, navigating the Arabian coast between Aden and the Persian Gulf required much respect due to the complete absence of light marks (with one exception, the light on Quoin Island in the entrance of the Gulf). Making things worse was the doubtful accuracy of available charts of that area at that time, some of the surveys dating back to the East India Trading Company days. (Some shipmasters were known to have their own ideas about the exact latitude and longitude of particular prominent marks shown on the charts, and would make pencil alterations, taking care to erase them when finally leaving the ship.) One salient and dangerous spot, Ras al Hadd, was the most easterly part of the coastline and at which the ship's course was a test and strain on a dark night in low visibility. (There used to be a story in circulation that some years previously a ship had run aground there and the whole crew slaughtered by the Arabs.) The Persian Gulf itself was not exactly an easy stretch of water to navigate either, due to the prevalence of sand storms during the heat of summer, also again the absence of lights except for one of very low power on a small island on our track at the lower end of the Gulf.

It was about a two-day run for our ships from the Quoins to the Shatt al Arab light vessel, where sometimes it would be necessary to anchor for sufficient water to cross the Bar. At such times, when the temperature could be 120° Fahrenheit in the shade, conditions became almost unbearable and we prayed for sunset. With the Iraqi pilot embarking from the spotless yacht-like pilot cutter we would eventually make our way up the Shatt al Arab river, becoming indifferent to the timeless spectacle of the canoe-like small craft plying their way among the date palms as of times immemorial. The river itself is fairly wide and winding, commencing with a kind of delta estuary and, with the land extremely low and flat. As can be seen on a map, its other end is the point where the rivers Tigris and Euphrates join.

The light brown water of the Shatt runs pretty swiftly and ships having to anchor in the Abadan (Bawarda) Reach frequently had to use the running or ordinary moor method. For some this would be seamanship-room knowledge, but for most B.T.C. men it was run of the mill practice.

The heat in that area was intense for a few months of the summer, when to swing a deck cargo valve without gloves during the day would burn the skin off your palms. Pages and covers of books curled up and went completely out of shape, whilst sliced bread placed on the table had to be covered with a damp napkin or else it would be like dried toast within minutes. At these times we slept in the 'nuddy' with just the sheet up in between our legs to cover the tummy. Fortunately there was an absence of mosquitoes due to the prevalence of oil. The local Gymkhana Club was the only place where Europeans could buy a cold drink, and being under the auspices of the Anglo Persian Oil Co. no cash was used – instead one used books of tickets in varying amounts of Rials, the local currency. It was well patronized by the ship's crews and those wanting to slake their thirst with cold beer, but officers were seldom able to get away from their duties, except on the rare occasions when having a night alongside with no cargo work.

Renewing acquaintanceships was a common probability at the Club on such occasions, the shore staff having been obliged to travel as passengers in the tankers. (Sophisticated air travel was still around the corner.) Most of the ships could carry up to twelve passengers, the busy season being the English winter months when wives would travel out to visit their husbands. It was referred to as the 'trooping season' and enjoyed by most officers as a pleasant diversion from the normally uneventful sea passages. It was one such run ashore that I bumped into Captain Commander at the Club, who, after the happy greeting, chided me for not accepting his offer of the sextant – of course it was a generous thought but not easily executed at the time of my dire need.

Looking back to those days although much is forgotten some of it will always stand the test of time – the endless sun glare on sand and water, the smell of crude oil, cargo preoccupations of specific gravities, temperatures, deadweight and drafts etc. Even with the 25% bonus East of Suez, the Company got their pound of flesh in exchange for the sixteen pounds stirling per month salary as a second mate. However I can recall feelings of being well employed by a good shipowner. The general complaint was that we were obliged to spend very long periods away from home.

One of the duties which gave me much interest and pleasure was that connected with the *British Duchess* being a Class B meteorological observing ship. Twice daily we were obliged to transmit a coded information message to the headquarters at Poona concerning sea and air temperatures, barometer readings, wind and force direction, sea and swell information together with the cloud formation. In turn we picked up other similar ship's coded messages enabling me to construct regular weather charts – knowing what weather lay ahead was always a great help to the chief officer's painting programme!

Interspersed with the Aden trips were cargoes to such other places as Karachi, Cochin, Columbo, Mombasa, Port Tewfik, Bombay, Madras and a memorable voyage to Cape Town during the Munich Crisis. At each of the two visits to Bombay to discharge cargo, the opportunity was taken to drydock the vessel. They were quick in and out jobs lasting no more than twenty-four hours, with crew changes as required.

Of high importance for selecting the crew was the serang, (bosun) of whom it was said would accept bribes from among the lucky ones picked – jobs were scarce. It appeared to me that mild corruption was a way of life with the Indian people; if a quartermaster was re-signing on the ship it would not be uncommon to find a little parcel of sweetmeats placed under the officer's pillow – their way of expressing gratitude for their jobs. The same play-acting was demonstrated at their special feast days (we called them 'hobson-jobson' days). In general we considered these seamen good and trustworthy, especially the petty officers, among them being the customary Chinese carpenter – referred to by the crew as china mistry sahib (not to be confused with burra 'mistry' sahib – the chief engineer). The captain was burra sahib – chief officer, burra malam sahib – second officer, do malam sahib, with the third officer or junior officer, chota malam sahib. They were very loyal people and I look back and think it was a privilege to serve among them; their pay was small by our standards, but compared with their fellow countrymen it was extremely good – some in the key positions on board could afford to buy an additional child-wife after only a two-year spell at sea!

The trip to Cape Town was quite a saga, commencing with the receiving of a W/T message during the first watch when about a day's run away with a cargo for Aden; I was asleep when somebody awakened me with the summons to report to the captain on the bridge. I noticed on the way up that the ship was heading in the opposite direction, which was explained when I was informed our orders were changed and that we were heading towards Cape Guardafui bound for Cape Town. Captain Goodchild wanted to know the estimated date of arrival at our changed destination, and it was as I started to open chart drawers that I realized we did not carry any charts of the southern hemisphere! Before returning to my bunk after a somewhat agitated discussion with the captain, the course was reversed again and the passage to Aden resumed. The intention was to collect a set of suitable charts, take on some fresh stores and

S.S. "BRITISH DUCHESS"
(All Percentages Minus From Engine Speed)
Table Of Differences (Percentage Form) Between Engine Speed And Speed Through W.

LOADED SHIP (Clean Bottom)

Wind between 3 points on either bow:-

Force	Sea	Difference	Foul Bottom
0	C	7%	10%
2	L	8%	11%
3	L	10%	12%
4	L—M	14%	14% *
5	M	20%	20% *
6	M—H	28%	28% *

Wind between 3 points & 6 Points, Either bow:-

Force	Sea	Difference	Foul Bottom
0	C	7%	10%
2	L	8%	11%
3	L	9%	12%
4	L—M	12%	12% *
5	M	17%	17% *
6	M—H	24%	24% *

Wind between 2 points before, and 5 points abaft either beam:-

Force	Sea	Difference	Foul Bottom
0	C	7%	10%
2	L	7%	10%
3	L	8%	11%
4	L—M	10%	11% *
5	M	14%	14% *
6	M—H	20%	20% *

Wind between 3 points on either quarter:-

Force	Sea	Difference	Foul Bottom
0	C	7%	10%
2	L	6%	9%
3	L	5%	8%
4	L—M	6%	9%
5	M	8%	11%
6	M—H	12%	12% *

(* = Unreliable)

LIGHT SHIP (Clean Bo

Wind between 3 points on either bow:

Force	Sea	Difference	Foul
0	C	3%	
2	L	5%	
3	L	6%	
4	L—M	8%	
5	M	14%	1
6	M—H	22%	2

Wind between 3 points & 6 pts., eithe

Force	Sea	Difference	Foul
0	C	3%	
2	L	5%	
3	L	6%	
4	L—M	7%	
5	M	12%	1
6	M—H	18%	1

Wind between 2 points before, and 5 abaft either beam:-

Force	Sea	Difference	Foul
0	C	2%	
2	L	2%	
3	L	3%	
4	L—M	5%	
5	M	9%	
6	M—H	15%	1

Wind between 3 points on either quar

Force	Sea	Difference	Foul
0	C	2%	
2	L	2%	
3	L	1%	
4	L—M	2%	
5	M	3%	
6	M—H	5%	

(* = Unreliable)

...ompiled this set of tables whilst serving as second officer. They are self-explanatory and worked reasonably well ...deep sea passages when sights were unobtainable, and when a dead-reckoning position was needed. What really ...ompts me to insert the table is the contrast with present day assistance and information available to the mariner. ...r example, a recent paper on Weather & Performance, with emphasis on ship resistance and the four major ...urces of speed reduction, giving details of the (1) frictional drag and water molecules (11) residuary drag and ...ip generated waves (111) wind resistance reduction. Final collation is then simplified by performance curves, ...d the reader will see the enormous advancement from the 10 knot days to present times – four or five decades

commence the long haul to Cape Town. During the middle watch however I started to think about the possibilities of making our own charts, and by the end of my watch when the chief officer came on the bridge to relieve me I felt it was a real possibility and we were soon in earnest discussion. Feeling very tired I eventually went below – the mate would speak to the captain after daylight. At one-bell when I went to the bridge to wind the chronometers it was to discover the ship had turned yet again and we were on an easterly course – it seemed the captain had been persuaded that it was possible to make suitable charts to see us safely down the east side of Africa.

Using the scale of charts in the northern hemisphere which corresponded to the latitudes through which we had to steam in the southern hemisphere, I selected the general chart of the Red Sea, and the Malta Straits to Syria as another. The backs of the cancelled charts were then used for the transfer of these two scales, after which the positions (latitudes and longitudes) of all salient points relevant to our courses through the Mozambique channel and round Cape Agulhas were plotted – a wealth of these points were listed in *Norie's Nautical Tables*, plus many more from the *Sailing Directions*. And so with this information, plus our combined local knowledge, three service-able charts were constructed as quickly as possible before the captain had time to change his mind about the inshore route (he had hinted there was always the alternative route down east of Madagascar – a perishing thought). All went well, I was proud of my chart construct-ing effort and Comoro Island was sighted spot on with our calculated position, giving all a boost of confidence. As fate would have it, the refrigerating plant broke down a day or two later and a large quantity of meat was thrown overboard, emphasizing how fortuitous it had been to select the inside route. The twenty-six day passage of six thousand or more miles was well embellished in the Cape Town paper *Cape Argus*, and although the reporting was slightly incorrect it was very gratifying and helped to fortify us on the long trek back to the Persian Gulf. At the same time we continued to listen to the news and speculate on Hitler's ambitions.

Some time prior to the Cape Town voyage the requisite sea time for sitting the master's certificate examination had been completed, and with this in view together with my eagerness to perform the initial Royal Naval Reserve training, application had been made for a transfer to one of the company's ships destined for a United Kingdom port. This came about on our return to Abadan from Cape Town, and I was transferred to the *British Councillor* on 12th November 1938.

Little of the short spell I served in the *'Councillor'* is remembered other than my signing off the vessel at Falmouth on 9th January 1939, and my haste to get home to my family, whom I had not seen for over two and a half years. After the emotional reunion I was handed a letter from the Union-Castle Line, saying my name was nearing the top of the waiting list if I were confirmed in my RNR rank!

At this stage of my career, I was twenty-five, under-weight according to the family doctor, about ten stone and not as physically fit as I might have been had I not spent so long in and around the Persian Gulf. Whether this had any effect on my determination I will never know for sure; I did however fail the seamanship part of the master's certificate examination and, instead of sitting that part again within a few weeks, decided to proceed with prearranged acceptance for the initial RNR training course which was due to commence within a week or so. (In retrospect I suppose there was an anxiousness to have the 'probationary acting' removed from my rank.) In due course the error of the timing of my actions became very evident as the later years will recount.

That of which I have written of pre-war life at sea so far has not included the two important events of the mid-thirties; I refer to the Spanish Civil War, and Italy's war against Abyssinia. The Mediterranean and Red Sea were both well used waters by the British Tanker Company's fleet and, the ships I served in during the pre-war period were no exceptions. For this reason the half century old period would not be complete without some reference to the increased activity in the Mediterranean brought about by the turmoil in Spain.

I was the junior officer of the *British General* which was discharging cargo at Oran on the Algerian coast when I was approached and invited to jump ship and accept a second mate's job running the blockade of Spain. They were offering a hundred pounds per month – a tempting offer compared with at the time eleven pounds odd per month. The exciting temptation remained clear in my mind for years. However, I must have had enough good sense to decline – loyalty and secure employment mattered in those days.

Knowledge of the International Brigade was very sketchy, we were always too busy to allow our thoughts to dwell on anything much other than our jobs. Any idle thoughts were usually of our constant desire for sleep.

Also taking place at this time was Benito Mussolini's war against Abyssinia; Italian troops had occupied Addis Ababa, with a great deal of sea transporting of soldiers and equipment between Italy and the

Southern Red Sea area. In spite of the introduction of sanctions imposed against Italy, my ship along with others of the company, were hard pressed supplying oil to Italy. The normal one, or possibly two, ports of discharge of a single cargo, had changed to as many as five ports of discharge for one cargo. This was hard work for the three deck officers of a 12,000-dwt ship, staying less than one day in each port. Cargo calculations, paper work, berthing and unberthing, and constant coastal navigation were all additional to the normal routine and brought about excessive strain for most of the ship's company. One such cargo loaded at Abadan in the Shatt al Arab was finally discharged at five Italian ports – Genoa, Leghorn, Naples, Messina and Venice. From this last port our ship was escorted out and clear of the harbour by two small gun boats, each with their guns trained on our bridge.

This final chapter of those pre-war times of Spanish and Italian warfare and then eventually the Munich Crisis, have been recorded by many professional and capable writers. However, the story of my life would not be complete without this insertion which is a suitable stepping stone to the Royal Naval part of my career which was to follow.

4. Into Battle

HMS *Ardent*

I commenced my Royal Naval Reserve long training early in May 1939 at HMS *Drake*, known to us as the Gunnery School Devonport. My destroyer time was served in *Ardent* – one of the Devonport Emergency Flotilla – and the work was hard, ranging paravanes and Fleet exercises.

H.M.S. Ardent

Ben Barker (Lt.Cdr.RN) was the driver and he came from a long line of the same calling. Always broke, blamed on his wife and five children, he will be remembered for his unorthodox rig when at sea. *Ardent* was lost off course when attacking the pocket battleship *Tirpitz* at Narvik. She was a happy ship and, later, when I found myself in the battleship *Revenge* I used to think back to those days, when we all knew each other well in the wardroom. It was also a comfort to have your fellow classmates dotted among the other ships of the flotilla because we were all so new to the Royal Navy. When ashore we tried to stick together.

Much of the flotilla's ships' companies were either new entrants or reservists, and the sea-training in gunnery, minesweeping and manoeuvres left little time to relax. When we finally passed out I

My fellow classmates

How we managed to form up our respective platoons on the parade ground, march to the Parade Commander, make a sword salute, return amidst the eyes of some hundreds of seamen and bark the order to stand your platoon at ease – was a mystery. We were only six officers in the Class 30 Y, as we were referred to; in the photograph can be seen the interwoven lace of which we were so proud. Wright, the only Lieutenant was in the flotilla leader Codrington, but the names of only two others can be remembered – Bird second from the left and Palastre third from the left, with myself second from the right.

The days of which I write are long gone, but I seem to remember Sub.Lieut. Palastre was in HMS Brazen, the most popular Party ship in the flotilla – many a Wren enjoyed becoming a 'brazen-girl'.

managed to scrape through with a third – I found weaponry and naval procedures all very new and complex after ten humdrum years trading to the Persian Gulf with the British Tanker Company Limited.

HMS *Revenge*

With only two weeks left, the training programme was stopped short, and we were appointed to ships in the Reserve Fleet, or to other sea-going units. Mine was to *Revenge*, then part of the second battle squadron in home waters. The life in a battleship was a far cry from that in barracks, or even destroyers, and I found it very testing. The main duties were quarterdeck officer of the watch in port and, at sea, bridge watch-keeping in an assistant capacity. There was never a quiet

A normal side-party comprising the petty officer of the watch at the gangway, then five ordinary seamen, next the bugler, the leading hand and marine corporal.

or dull moment at either of these duties, and a moment of day-dreaming could cost one dearly.

Similar to an old fashion telephone exchange, nothing seemed to happen on board without the officer of the watch on the quarter-deck being concerned. When I joined it was amid much activity as *Revenge* prepared to join the Reserve Fleet Review at Weymouth. One quickly discovered the officer to look out for was the commander (Biggs – later to become Flag Officer I believe) who kept us very much on our toes.

As with most large naval units, a converted North Sea drifter was attached to *Revenge* for the purpose of landing/returning libertymen and transporting stores. Ours was called *Mist* and she soon became my charge. Looking back and studying notes, press cuttings and photographs one realizes there seems no limit to what the mind and body is capable of at that age, and my introduction to *Revenge* seemed kaleidoscopic to say the least. The gathering of 130 ships of the Reserve Fleet at short notice was no mean task, emphasized in the King's message to the Fleet: "The bringing forward for sea service of so many ships in a few days proves how smoothly the organisation works, and leaves no doubt in my mind that the Fleet will quickly reach a high standard of fighting efficiency".

Revenge was one of the three battleships present. The others were *Ramilles and Iron Duke*, together with the carrier *Courageous*. We were stationed on the seaward perimeter of 14 columns of warships ranging from MTBs, mine-sweepers, submarines, destroyers and cruisers. It was a most impressive sight on 9th August 1939 as the King sped along the columns of spick-and-span ships in the royal barge (as I write this and study a photograph of the cruiser *HMS Dunedin* with the King and entourage speeding past, I remember the emphatic instructions from the commander to keep the drifter out of sight of the royal barge!) Far from any feelings of humiliation, we carried on until the late hours of the night, first landing, and then returning the 10,000 libertymen who had in various ways enjoyed their special run ashore.

Officer of the watch on board Revenge, back in port at anchor after one of the frequent working-up exercises in the English Channel, The small telescope under my arm was merely a customary kind of badge of office. It required a dexterously quick movement to salute and at the same time have the instrument gripped firmly in the left hand – it came with practice.

The drifter HMS *Mist*

And so life in *Revenge* went on. We worked hard and from time to time played hard, but in the back of our minds we were aware of the possibilities ahead, and the dialogue between our country and Germany. There never seemed to be much advanced notice of anything, so that on the day the commander told me to select three snotties (midshipmen) from the gun room to assist, and take *Mist* to Scapa Flow, came as a surprise. With sailing orders instructing me to make for the nearest port in the event of a declaration of war, we joined company with the drifter *Sheen* belonging to the *Resolution* and in the charge of a Sub.Lt. RN from the cruiser HMS *Cardiff.* He had the assistance of two Midshipmen, making a total complement of seventeen in each drifter. Passage was commenced the following morning and it was suggested *Mist* would lead the way.

My three snotties, Scott, Westmacott, and Vance, were young men of great vitality, each of whom I was destined to meet again. Our first stop was Milford Haven for provisions and fuel, to carry on the next day up the Irish Sea and west-about in accordance with the sailing orders. We cast off at daybreak in a flat calm with the ominous absence of wind. Half way down the Sound visibility was zero; astern of us the *Sheen*'s whistle became fainter until it could be heard no more. Creeping slowly along we ran St Ann's Head fog signal abeam then stopped, hoping *Sheen* would catch up. Suddenly several whistles were heard to seaward just as the fog was beginning to thin out, and then I saw the Milford trawler, coming straight at us with a bone in its teeth. Fortunately all hands were above deck, otherwise the trawler's stem would have killed or injured anybody down below at the time of the collision. Although making water we managed to make Milford Dock entrance safely. Completing the sorry story was news that the *Sheen* had lost her anchor whilst seeking an anchorage in the fog.

It was several days before *Mist* completed repairs, and the small fishing port held little attraction for our men, although it did give to myself the opportunity of visiting the little town of Narbeth, in Pembrokeshire, where I had spent my boyhood.

Half-way up the Irish Sea the telegraphist reported that a state of war had been declared so we made tracks for Belfast. Once again we topped up with fuel and provisions and with the all-important recognition signals collected, we were ready to proceed. In the middle of completing these requirements the sub. of *Sheen* was recalled to his ship leaving myself in charge of the operation. Scott was put in charge of the other drifter and the feelings of increased responsibility became apparent. The instructions from the N.O.I.C. were to sail at a specified time when the channel buoys would be lighted for thirty minutes, but midshipman Vance was not on board *Mist* or the *Sheen* when the sailing time came. Facing up to the business of making important decisions, we remained alongside and sent a search party to town where Vance had last been seen. It was well past our sailing time when our friend was escorted back aboard – allegedly torn from an amorous encounter. Braving the blackness of the strange channel, with Scott obediently keeping close astern, the passage to the open waters became a series of gentle groundings as we groped our way along the winding waterway. It was a relief to reach deeper water and in the darkness *Mist* was obliged to anchor in order that *Sheen* could secure alongside whilst she removed mud and sand from her tubes. Fortunately our main engine in *Mist* was diesel, but *Sheen* had to rely on a steam boiler. It was breaking day before all was in order for us to proceed on our way, in my case with a feeling of elation at overcoming our difficulties unbeknown by the local authorities. Later I was to discover those feelings were illfounded.*

With the course set for the Mull of Kintyre in the North Channel, there was a certain concern because of the recent sinking by a U-Boat of the *Athenia* in the North Western Approaches, and our orders to proceed west of the Outer Hebrides. (I wondered if my superiors thought the Inner Hebrides route would be too tricky to navigate – I was never to know the answer.) A decision was made to go through the Caledonian Canal and on we steamed, inside the Isle of Islay and up the Firth of Lorne. It was a pitch dark night when we reached the lower end of Loch Linnhe, so we anchored with *Sheen* once again alongside.

For much of the night I lay awake listening to the movement of the anchor chain and the occasional barking of a dog on the nearby bank. (The water in the Loch was so deep we had some anxious moments anchoring so close to the land.) Daylight came and we successfully negotiated the forbidding entrance to Loch Linnhe, to arrive off Fort William when the day was still young. There was no lack of interested local helpers for manning the capstan bars needed to operate the lock gates, it being fairly evident the White Ensign was an unfamiliar sight in those parts.

We were well under way along the first leg of our passage through the canal (Loch Loggan) before the absence of Midshipman Vance was realized, and a message flashed to *Sheen* confirmed he was not there either. He was last seen helping to turn one of the capstans at Fort William. It was decided to keep on going until we reached Inverness, when this new development would then be dealt with.

The lock entrance Fort William

To say our passage was interesting would be an under statement; the Lochs were rather dark and gloomy, but the actual canal-way provided some tight bends to tax our attention, particularly one evening when it became dark before reaching the safety of the next Loch. This was Fort Augustus, where Scottish

Towards the end of January 1940 when I was recovering from the dissection of my tonsils, I discovered quite by chance from a fellow patient that the incident at Belfast concering the Mist *and* Sheen, *was closely followed by the port authority and a report given to the N.O.I.C.*

hospitality was provided by the lo-cal regiment stationed there. Loch Ness was very forbidding, with no sighting of the monster to relieve the monotonous scenery.

In due course we arrived safely at Inverness, where our friend Vance returned on board his ab-sence always having remained a complete mystery.

After the formalities with the harbour master were completed, we proceeded into the Moray Firth on the last leg of the adventure.

By the time we were approach-ing Dunscansby Head the *Sheen* had dropped a long way astern and we were obliged to ease down.

The bridge of HMS Mist

This cost us the favourable tide crossing the Pentland Firth and it was getting dark by the time we reached the boom across the entrance to Scapa Flow. We were given the option of staying outside until next morning or entering between the western end of the boom and the rocks. In the failing light we successfully completed that manoeuvre. *Mist* was ordered to berth alongside HMS *Royal Oak* and *Sheen* alongside the *Iron Duke*.*

One day succeeded another as the *Mist* was engaged transport-ing stores and other duties.We wondered when our return to *Revenge* would take place; with the war newly started we thought we might have been overlooked.

The day came when our small ship's company was issued with railway warrants for our return, but my departure was somewhat different; I was to escort a senior officer who was suffering from neurasthenia down to Haslow Hospital in the south of England. Taking charge of both railway tickets, with instructions to keep a close but tactful eye on him, we crossed to Thurso and commenced the journey. Alone together in the first class compartment, the train had covered several miles before the officer suddenly leaned forward and said "I suppose you think I'm mad don't you"–what could a rooky sub. lieut. say to that? He went on to tell me the story of how during the 1914-1918 war he was stationed at Scapa Flow for two years, he found the lonliness unbearable and vowed he would never do it again.

* *Very soon after this interlude at Scapa Flow the German U-Boat Ace Prien managed to enter Scapa undetected and sink the* Royal Oak. *I often wondered whether Prien's entrance to the Flow had been negotiated at the same time as our two drifters.*

As time passed I became reassured of his wellbeing. At Invergordon we visited the paymaster to draw cash, and spent the night at an hotel in Inverness. Another stop was made at Edinburgh where we stayed two days before carrying on to London, then finally after several delays we reached our destination, and I was free to report back to *Revenge*.

Return to *Revenge*

There was much activity going on when eventually I did reach *Revenge*, small wooden cases were being loaded and stowed in X magazine. To satisfy our curiosity we were told they were gas filled shells! The next day we steamed out into the Channel and headed westward. No doubt certain senior officers on board knew what was going on and what was planned but the junior officers thought it was just another exercise in the channel.

We continued westward well past the point of normal return. Later that evening, as the old battleship continued on a westerly course with her sharp stem dipping into the swell, Captain Archer our commanding officer broadcast over the intercom that *Revenge* was bound for Halifax in Nova Scotia. (There would have been a score of disappointed and heart broken people in Weymouth that night.) In due course we arrived at Halifax, and the mysterious boxes were brought up from the magazine and off loaded – we had carried a large portion of the gold from the Bank of England!

Halifax became the new base of operations and, together with HMS *Resolution* we carried out sweeps over the North Atlantic, hoping for (or fearing) an encounter with the German raider Deutschland. We were constantly in some state of readiness for action and it was absolutely necessary for every man on board to know his correct station in each of these states of readiness. This vital piece of information was kept up to date and easily accessible, on the watch and quarter bill. Visits to our sleeping quarters were rare and the business of keeping shaved and washed was always a problem. During first degree of readiness my action station was the armoured tower just abaft B turret under the bridge. It was a wet and cold position, a complete contrast from the Persian Gulf where I had spent most of my sea-time. There was much speculation about the possibility of action. the German pocket battleships with their eleven inch guns had a much faster rate of fire than our fifteen inch four twin turrets. However, visibility in the North Atlantic is seldom extreme so much of our exercise was for a low visibility sudden encounter, for which the term "Rammer Archer – the Atlantic Ghost" was coined for the commanding officer – *Revenge* having a ram on the stem's forefoot. These sweeps were cut short when the second Canadian expeditionary force was transported across the North Atlantic by troopships with *Revenge* as the surface escort.

It was an uneventful passage except towards the end as we entered the Firth of Clyde, when there was a submarine contact by an escorting destroyer. In the excitement Captain Archer ordered an emergency turn. I was the assistant officer of the bridge watch (voice-pipe number) and at the precise moment of repeating an order to the wheelhouse below I experienced a spasm of coughing (tonsillitis).Very little escaped the captain's notice and soon after we were safely anchored off Gourock I was despatched to the Naval Hospital at Devonport for the tonsillectomy operation.

HMS *Revenge*

HMS Revenge *leaving Portsmouth on 29th August 1939 after an unscheduled visit, where she had completely topped up her magazines. She is a grand sight with her sides manned – about four hundred of the complete complement being Royal Naval Reserves like myself.*
Her armament of four twin fifteen inch guns, the battery of ten six-inch and two twin 4.2 inch HA/LA guns just abaft the bridge was her contribution towards the business of preserving peace.
The round dome just under the bridge looking like a large inverted basin immediately abaft B turret, was the armoured tower which held the fifteen inch control equipment. It was a secondary position for use in the event of the main top position of control, sited well above the bridge, being put out of action. It was my action station in first degree.

5. Interlude

East Moyra

In the chapter concerning HMS *White Bear* mention was made of delivering a motor launch from Plymouth to Milford Haven. Because this took place whilst assigned to the Devonport Barracks for general duties, it is considered appropriate to relate the story at this time. *East Moyra* was a fine little craft, but essentially for inshore waters rather than a winter passage around Land's End. There was a man to look after the engine, also a deckhand, both known as T 124 crew (my first reaction when seeing it was to wonder why it could not have been sent to Milford by road transport)! It was needed for naval boarding purposes in the Haven so, with few instructions and a supply of contingency money, off we went on 9th February 1940 with the weather fair for the time of the year.

Our first stop was Falmouth late that afternoon for the necessary fuel, food and rest, then carrying on the next morning making for Penzance. Apart from a low swell it was a windless day and we had not reached the Lizard when a periscope was seen about fifty yards away on our beam. The identification was shared by the deckhand in the cockpit at the time, although the sighting could only have lasted about one minute as the launch ranged up and down in the swell. Needless to say the sole topic was the submarine periscope as we covered the remaining distance to Newlyn, where we tied up in the harbour and I made for the nearby public telephone. The sighting report was made to an officer on duty in the office of the chief of staff at Mount Wise, Plymouth. I will always remember part of the acknowledgement: "Are you sure it wasn't a broom-handle". The fair weather held and the next morning we were on our way again, this time hoping to make Newquay. Crossing St.Ives Bay the engine broke down and it was beyond our capabilities to repair. With no communication facilities other than small flags, a distress signal was rigged and hoisted in the hope a sharp-eyed Coastguard would spot it. The danger was that with the wind and tide we would drift inshore onto the bar at Hayle. After what seemed an age, with the long furrows of Hayle bar getting too close for comfort, we saw the St.Ives lifeboat come out of the harbour and head for us. We were soon taken in tow and our anxiety ended. As we tied up at the harbour wall, the coxswain explained the reason for the delay. There was little doubt we were very lucky that day because it appeared the St.Ives lifeboat disaster of 18th January 1939 (all hands lost) had left the station without a lifeboat. The replacement, called *Caroline Oates Aver,* had only just arrived a day or so before, together with the tractor for hauling it across the harbour sand at low water. There were some problems getting the tractor operational for the very first time so the lifeboat had to be

East Moyra *under tow by* Caroline Oates Aver

manhandled across the sand until it was afloat.

Eight days passed before finally the necessary engine spare parts were obtained and fitted, during which time I stayed at a private hotel and enjoyed the Cornish hospitality. So it was with a feeling of regret when on 20th February 1940 we resumed our passage along the North Cornish coast, making for Padstow. Just before we left the next morning we heard on the radio that a tanker called *Caroni River* had struck a mine outside Falmouth the previous day, injuring some of the shipyard workers. It was subsequently discovered that a minefield had been laid and, as far as we were concerned that was a distinct connection with the submarine periscope we had seen.

Leaving Padstow behind, our thoughts were concentrated on the next place of call. The bar outside Appledore looked distinctly unpleasant so we carried on through Bideford Bay and around to Ilfracombe, which we reached just before darkness set in. It was a Saturday night and we felt a suitable time for departure would be Monday morning, weather permitting. I put up at a hotel overlooking the harbour. The proprietor was an ex-London first division soccer player, who together with his wife made my short stay very enjoyable. We left as planned and the last leg of the venture was completed safely by late afternoon on 24th February 1940, when we secured in Milford Dock – fifteen days after leaving Plymouth.

HMS *White Bear*

It was said that White Bear was offered, by her wealthy American owner, to the British Government as a war effort contribution. Her name at the time was Iolanda and she was the largest yacht afloat. However it was before the U.S.A. entered the war and the neutrality laws presented a problem, so she was sold to us for one dollar. Built in Southampton by Camper & Nichlson, probably in the twenties, she was made of iron and rust was never in evidence. Everything was of superb quality, and workmanship was of the highest standard. With twin screw she needed skilful handling in the heavy weather we had to contend with around the Orkneys and Shetlands.

My daughter was christened on board White Bear in 1941, the large ship's bell having been unshipped specially from its tabernacle for use as the font. This ceremony took place in Holy Loch during one of our periodic boiler cleans, the padre from HMS Maidstone (depot ship of the submarine flotilla) officiating. She was named Deirdre after a legendary beautiful woman who lived in the hills surrounding Holy Loch and who used to haunt the men with her charms.

HMS *White Bear*

After a spot of sick leave, recuperating from the tonsillectomy, a temporary appointment, was served at HMS *Drake,* the R.N. barracks. In due course I was to be returned to *Revenge,* but the thought gave me little pleasure, so I put a request in to serve in small ships. The time went by and I was kept busy on the general duties of the barracks; from issuing bloomers to new Wrens, to taking a six ton cabin launch from Plymouth to Milford Haven. But in due course my appointment came through to join *White Bear.* The sight of a 2,000-ton yacht was a staggering surprise, I expected it to be some kind of trawler.

In the ship's peacetime role my quarters had been a guest cabin. It was still luxuriously appointed, complete with en suite bathroom, double bed and exquisite french-style pieces of fitted furniture. The colour scheme, according to my new wife, was pale blue and dove grey. There was a long lever-style handle beside the toilet, and a foot peddle on the floor, with a printed notice on the bulkhead saying "*Twelve full strokes with the foot pressed down*".

Having shed the probationary/acting, I was now a fully fledged Sub-Lieutenant with a permanent commission in the Royal Naval Reserve – my watch-keeping certificate having been obtained in *Revenge*. Performing general duties I soon settled in with my fellow officers. Another sub-lieut. RNR by the name of Tait (ex Union-Castle) was the navigating officer, Cooper, a lieut. RNVR, was the first lieutenant and we got along well under the command of the four-ringed Captain, RNR Roy Gill.

Captain Gill later became Commodore whilst still on the active list – and later still Sir Roy Gill K.B.E. At the time it was claimed he was the first RNR officer to reach the rank of commodore on the

Myself, now a Lieutenant, standing on the quarterdeck at about the spot where my daughter was christened.

active list. It was further alleged that when put to the Monarch that Gill would possibly have to be placed on the retired list as a rear admiral, the reply was "We don't want 'Pink Admirals' in our Navy".

White Bear at this time was attached to the 2nd Submarine Flotilla based in Scotland; we saw a great deal of Rosyth, Dundee and, as the war progressed, Holy Loch on the Clyde. Our job was two-fold, to exercise with our submarines to the point of being fully operational and trained, then to escort them individually through the sanctuaries to the starting points of their patrols which were usually north of the Shetlands. It was hard work, with no let up as the new submarines were being commissioned. They were mostly in the hands

My wife Rita with Deirdre

of young and dedicated lieutenants, who fired their dummy torpedoes at us and played other war games. It was always with a kind of personal sense of relief that our submarine would surface at the edge of the rendezvous area as scheduled, and be led safely back to the mother ship for their well earned rest and replenishment.

After a while Tait left to join the submarine service, and I took over as navigating officer. Atlantic convoys were having their casualties; Commodore Gill was appointed to this vital service and made his contribution in the Battle of the Atlantic. His departure was a sad day and things seemed to change after he left us. The well ploughed waters of the inshore route around Scotland lost some of their excitment and fascination for me so I applied for convoy escort work.

After the prerequisite further Asdic courses were completed I was sent to HMS *Wanderer* for first lieutenant's training. I never saw *White Bear* again but, for a long time afterwards I used to recall the midnight submerging of our charges after the last blue lamp flashed message "Good luck and good hunting".

My time in *White Bear* came to an end in 1942 when I was appointed First Lieutenant of HMS *Aubretia* – my first Flower class corvette.

HMS White Bear *in her glory before being sold to the British Government at the outbreak of the second world war. Opened to commercial shipping in 1914, the Panama Canal is here seen with the finishing touches in progress.*

6. North Atlantic Convoys

HMS *Wanderer*

My introduction during January 1942 to the North Atlantic convoy escort work was short and sharp to say the least. It came after a short Asdic course when I reported to the old "W" class destroyer HMS *Wanderer* at Londonderry. She was a group leader under the command of Commander Orpin RN and my temporary appointment was the first lieutenant training. Time in port was minimal during those days of escort shortage, and hardly before being able to grasp one thing from another we were off to the rendezvous point of a west bound convoy of some ninety-odd merchant ships forming in the North Western Approaches. The weather was foul, a typical Western Ocean westerly gale force wind giving me my first taste of these slender sharp pointed ships ploughing through and under the heavy seas. There was little protection and for days on end our clothes were damp or soaking wet.

In all states of readiness I was assigned the duty of officer of the bridge watch or the assistant of such. This meant most of the time not sleeping. My position would be on the bridge, this was the best place to learn what would be required of a first lieutenant of an A/S convoy escort vessel. My sleeping quarters was a camp-bed on the deck of the captain's cabin. Most of the time an inch or so of sea water was sloshing about with the violent movements of the ship. In all the years I spent at sea, nothing so uncomfortable and dangerous was ever experienced.

The convoy was made up of the usual medium size ocean going merchant ships with the speed set for about ten knots, whilst the other escorts of the group were corvettes, except for one armed deepsea trawler stationed astern of the columns, its main purpose being to retrieve survivors from any crippled ship of the convoy. The position of *Wanderer* was ahead of the convoy and all ships were performing the prescribed zig-zag. There was never a dull moment and every man was constantly alert throughout the ship, including lookouts, guns' crews, asdic, signalmen, telegraphists, wheelhouse crew, engine-room and other less conspicuous stations all coping with the rain squalls and constant signals from the commodore. There would be course alterations, rounding up stragglers, bad station keeping and many other things of vital importance. Although the German U-Boat packs had not properly got under way at that time, the danger from single submarines was present at all times both day and night.

On the chance that a U-Boat was shadowing a convoy by day, waiting to make her attack when darkness came, it was customary soon after darkness fell for the commodore of the convoy to signal by blue lamp a course alteration in order to make it difficult for the U-Boat to position herself for the effective firing of her torpedoes.

It was during one of these course alterations one night, when the gale which had blown for days had started to ease off, although there was still heavy cloud and intermittent rain, when *Wanderer's* signalman failed to read the new course which the convoy was to turn to at the specified time. We decided to close the leading ships of the columns after the alteration time and steam across the path of the convoy taking bearings of the leading ships. During this drawn out procedure, with the commanding officer and first lieutenant's eyes glued to the compass rose, I, as assistant OOW concentrated doubly on a sharp lookout ahead. At first I thought the faint light from a half moon behind the lowering clouds was making my eyes play tricks. Then I was sure. It was a U-Boat on the surface bearing about five degrees on our port bow and heading towards us. My yell "U-Boat ahead" galvanized everyone, and with urgent shouts from the C.O. "Where-where". His night vision was temporary lost through peering at the compass, and I kept pointing at the submarine as the range quickly

HMS Wanderer *refuelling at sea at a later date than the period described in the forgoing narrative, when we were not fitted with the RDF (Radar) tower, the funnels were slender and "A" gun was still fitted. Otherwise she was the same 'narrow gutted greyhound' with her open bridge and dangerously exposed after-deck.*

closed. At the same time I performed the duties which would motivate the crew with their weapons.

Within seconds the well oiled drill was working, but by the time the orders were given and responded to, the commanding officer had seen the submarine. It had reached the inside of our turning circle and our effort to ram failed as she crash dived. With the green seas coming over the *Wanderer*'s stem, the 4" B-Gun's crew could not depress low enough for effective use, so that the only surface weapon to find the target was the short-range pom-pom, which although exploding on the U-Boat's hull as she sank below the surface would have done very little damage. What effect the pattern of depth charges had when fired we were never to know, but having skirted within fifty yards of the diving position when they were fired it is possible some damage was inflicted.

I am unable to print the comments of Commander Orpin as the submarine was lost to sight under the waves, and I will always have those lurking doubts as to whether I should have taken the initiative to ram the U-Boat when first identified. As for the convoy, what its fate would have been had we not fortuitously encountered the submarine is left to the imagination – the havoc could have been tremendous. As it was, with the submarine alarm having been made to the convoy and escorts, *Wanderer* carried on. We were never to know for sure the fate of the U-Boat — the trawler astern of the convoy would have been in the ideal position to make contact and destroy, or she may have survived to return to her base, and maybe provide Lord Haw-Haw more fictitious claims of destruction to our war effort.

Mid ocean meeting point (MOMP) half way across the Atlantic was reached in due course and the convoy intact handed over to the American escort force. Our group rendezvoused with an east-bound convoy and, with the wind and seas now astern, welcomed the relief as we zig zagged our return to U.K. waters.

HMS *Aubretia*

After my short but hectic stay in *Wanderer*, I was quickly appointed as first lieutenant to *HMS Aubretia*, a Flower class corvette, and so it was back on the North Atlantic convoy escort work again.

Under the command of Lieut. Cdr. Funge-Smith, RNR, we were attached to a group based at Moville in Northern Ireland. The constant demands on each ship of the group left very little time for relaxation. In those days the leader was invariably a RN officer and the corvette's total ship's company of eighty or ninety strove hard to keep up the required standard expected of a major war vessel. One of the sub.lieuts. was also RNR and by coincidence he, like the C.O. and myself, were peacetime officers in the same shipping company.

Conditions in a corvette were not exactly pleasant and there were times when our spray or rain soaked bodies took some severe treatment as the ship punched, pitched or rolled in her zig-zagging progress of keeping the convoy in some order of shape.

HMS Aubretia *at Gourock early in 1942*

A change came with *Aubretia* forming part of an escort force assigned to a Sierra Leone convoy; it was a welcome relief to feel the warm sun again, and even the baptismal affects of oiling at sea failed to dampen our spirits with the prospects of a spell of service in warmer waters. By the time we reached single figure latitudes men's bodies had changed from white through red to brown, and our single sick-berth attendant had started to enjoy some relief from treating sore backs.

We reached Freetown harbour in due course and became part of the local escort force. Our duties were mainly meeting the Sierra Leone convoys in the vicinity of 20 degrees North, remaining with them until reaching the Equator where the ships would be dispersed at the nearest midnight. This twelve hundred or so miles of the West African coast had its variations of duties, and although sometimes likened to 'stink-holes', places like The Gambia and Ivory Coast certainly had some unusual sights to offer.

Merchant Navy survivors presented a problem for small naval vessels with their small cramped spaces, and the single marauding U-

Boat was a constant danger. Sometimes a ship falling foul of a torpedo would have particular significance, such as the *Muncaster Castle* which was the leading ship of the port column before dispersal and abreast of which *Aubretia* had taken station. We subsequently sank two of her lifeboats by gunfire, but before doing so removed the useful equipment (I still have the shipwright's brace from one of the empty boats).

Life was never dull and from time to time there were always incidents. Early one morning, returning independently to Freetown from the Equator, and shortly after the horizon became visible in the early light, a ship partly hull-down was sighted ahead. Within a couple of minutes it was identified as a large passenger ship independently routed, and probably carrying troops en-route to North Africa via the Cape and Red Sea. Suddenly the vessel turned and disappeared below the horizon. Soon our telegraphist picked up a submarine sighting broadcast giving a position, which on transfer to the chart gave our exact latitude and longitude at the time the troopship turned away. From ten or twelve miles the old RDF tower abaft the bridge of a corvette could easily give the appearance of a submarine conning tower, so we made a signal to the C. in C. West Africa explaining the situation. After a pause we received a reply: "Remain in the vicinity for twenty-four hours and carry out search for submarine".

In between convoys or patrols, life and conditions in Freetown were pretty much what one would expect under the watchful eyes of the destroyer depot-ship and the captain. Never ending reports and signals with much boat activity was normal, plus of course our times of relaxation when the "R-P-C" (request [the] pleasure [of your] company) and "W-M-P" (with much pleasure – the phrase used to accept the R-P-C invitation) system went into top gear. Ashore there was a canteen where 'Jack' could sweat out the beer as fast as it was consumed. The hospital ship *Oxfordshire* on permanent station was never without a good quota of malaria patients, and for a short while I was unfortunate enough to be one of them. There were few regrets when in late 1942 *Aubretia* developed boiler trouble and an end to the sweating and sweet potatoes was in sight, as we took station on the screen of a U.K. bound convoy.

Some weeks later at a repair yard in the Thames and after our commanding officer's promotion I was given the opportunity to take over *Aubretia*, or alternatively undergo special hospital out-patient treatment for the malaria. Making the decision was extremely difficult, and I think the state of being newly married with a young child must have had some influence upon my regretful leaving of *Aubretia*.

7. Mobile Anti-Submarine Training Unit

The attack of malaria I contracted in West Africa was quite severe, sufficiently so that for the most part of a convoy operation I was unable to perform my duties, even to the extent of not being aware of what was taking place around me – and later when placed aboard the hospital ship my state of health was considered quite seriously low. So it was obviously with this knowledge in mind that I decided to seek further medical attention when leaving my appointment of first lieutenant of HMS *Aubretia*.

I was sent to Newton Abbot Hospital where tests were carried out, resulting in a special course of medication being prescribed concurrent with being unfit for sea service for a period of twelve months.

With the German submarine warfare taking its heavy toll on our convoys, it was not surprising that I was quickly reappointed and soon found myself at HMS *Osprey* in Scotland – the anti-submarine training establishment, where I commenced a seven weeks' course. There they taught the operating procedure of the various anti-submarine detecting devices along with the tactics used by attacking U-Boats. In addition there was emphasis on the tactical equipment (simulators), a prerequisite to the completion of the course and the assignment to taking charge of *MASTU 9*, a mobile unit operating on the east coast of Scotland under the administration of the C. in C. Rosyth, but still on the books of *Osprey*.

Having my wife and child safely installed with the wife of Commodore Gill near Dunfermline, I felt very lucky to have this shore appointment and, although the unit *MASTU 9* was merely a single decker bus and bore no resemblance to an escort vessel, we were nevertheless concerned with the same aspect of the war. With only two for a crew, the driver who was an higher submarine detector together with a petty officer telegraphist, my purpose was to supervise the training programme issued by the C. in C's asdic office. This included keeping asdic teams up to date with changes to the operating procedure and imparting certain classified information. Our usual routine would be to select a spot within the naval controlled area where electrical power was available and unload the transformer from the parked unit which provided the 110-volt power necessary for operating the tactical table. These preparations were timed to conform with the training programme circulated among the escort vessels in the area, and the necessary test runs were always completed by the time the first ship's team arrived. The tactical table produced a synthetic submerged submarine together with the surface anti-submarine vessel; the submarine was controlled by the P.O. and the surface vessel in hands of the team's C.O. Realistic U-Boat tactics would be depicted to test the operating standard of the asdic ratings and team's skill. Most of the ships we were concerned with were of the Dance class trawler, but there were the converted types too, with other escort vessels undergoing refit in Scotish ports. Usually the C.O. plus asdic officer and all the ships asdic ratings would attend these absorbing sessions, with keen interest being so obviously connected to the real thing they had experienced, or hoped to encounter at sea. The climatic point where the pattern of depth charges would explode was always tense and realistic, and the subsequent postmortem produced complete attention from every member of the team as the tracings of the submarine and attacking ship were studied, explained and lessons learned.

Many friends were made among the ships and shore establishments between Newcastle and Dundee, especially those of the fishing fraternity, and the odd fish or pheasant never came amiss. Infrequently the more remote and isolated places would be included – one such place was the small quaint fishing port of Anstruther on the north side of the entrance to the Firth of Forth, where the defence included a fixed asdic beam. So the grey painted bus became a familiar sight parked on numerous docksides, and it was hardly surprising as my interest grew with the exercises, that after some time the thoughts of returning to sea with the newly acquired knowledge grew apace, and when during 1943 an acting half-stripe was shipped, the end of the twelve month period was awaited with keen anticipation.

One of the temporary assignments meted out after handing over the unit was being sent to Falmouth, where for several weeks I acted as hardmaster with an American counterpart. With this lieutenant our duties were to supervise the loading and unloading of L.S.T. and L.C.T. invasion exercises. A *hard* had been constructed in the Helford Passage – a very remote and secluded spot and ideal for the concealment of the vast quantity of war equipment. The daily exercises with these landing craft on the hard was of course a prelude to D-Day, which finally came on 6th June 1944 and just about the time of my departure from the Clyde in the troopship *Orion*, along with some five thousand other miscellaneous types destined for the pursuance of the war in Eastern parts – in my case to take over command of HMS *Genista*.

8. The Middle East

HMS *Genista*

I was one of a dozen or so RN, RNR, and RNVR officers who became passengers on board the troopship *Orion* anchored in the Clyde some time in 1944. We were some five thousand miscellaneous service people destined for India in pursuance of the continuation of the war further East.

The women services were well represented, among whom were twenty or so Wren officers, who completely brightened the tedious aspect of a wartime troopship passage – one RN lieutenant even fell for a trim third officer Wren under the effects of Red Sea evenings and pulsating boat decks under cloudless planetary skies. They married on arrival in Bombay.

Orion made a fuel stop at Aden and, through the bush telegraph I discovered that my new command, *Genista*, was somewhere in the vicinity. The O.C. Troops, a dugout naval commander, was uncooperative about my request to get off there and then, rather than carry on to Bombay. So I resigned myself to the remaining few days and in due course landed in Bombay. During the trip I became quite friendly with another officer whose appointment was similar to mine, so we both became very frustrated when we found ourselves shunted up country to a place called Chumba, a transit camp miles from anywhere. The place had the appearance of being recently established and to say the least it was very primitive.

It was hot and sticky that first night as we tried to sleep and by dawn the decision to literally escape, was clear. Still very early the astonished Indian was too surprised to argue when we threw our gear into his Bombay bound lorry and climbed in after it. Eventually we rattled to a stop in some smelly suburb, boarded a taxi with orders to tour the docks until we found the ship we were looking for. I felt sure we could cadge a trip back to Aden on the leader of the escort which had brought us across the Arabian Sea. The C.O.'s nickname was 'Wolf' and we were acquaintances from Moville days. I think that any lack of naval knowledge in those days was made up for in initiative among rookies. In this particular case Wolf's reply to our request was "I certainly won't see you two coming aboard at 0800 hours tomorrow morning". The group of three frigates made a swift passage back to Aden and in no time it seemed I was in *Genista* entering the harbour on completion of the weekend take-over routine, that being the official moment I took over command. A launch had taken my predecessor ashore and I was busy remembering all the advice I had been given about approaching our berth and securing. Putting it mildly the operation turned out to be a complete lashup – an exercise which locally the ships liked to complete in five minutes, took *Genista* over an hour. The subsequent postmortem disclosed that my voice was too loud; having given the order to the seaboat's crew, 'Slip', the stoker P.O. on the forcastle also jumped into action and let go the anchor! I shall never forget my feelings of that malfunctioned operation – the eyes of a dozen ships plus the naval base watching the pantomime. Typical of the naval rating, it was not long before the dog-watches were punctured with a composition to the tune of the 'Strawberry Blonde', the refrain going "The Skipper did drip as he swung round the ship – and the lads smiled on".

Genista was actually based in Kilindini, East Africa, but did regular ninety day stints working from Aden. The tasks varied from 'escorting' to sweeps across the Gulf of Aden and Arabian Sea, even to an undignified towing of an LCM from Salalah to Djibouti. I remember the elaborate towing bridle made up by the chief bosun's mate, which parted the first night at sea. Not wanting to lose the tow in the darkness a four and a half inch berthing wire eye was tossed aboard. Soon we were obliged to steam very slowly ahead, and very soon found we had the LCM riding comfortably on the quarter, and remained so at about seven knots to our destination. It seemed to raise no eyebrows in my special report. Well, this hum-drum routine was

HMS *Genista*

47

curtailed when *Genista*, with the escorts *Freesia* and *Falmouth* in company were detailed to escort the battleship *Valiant* (a lame duck) down to Durban, via Kilindini, where we were joined by two small passenger ships carrying miscellaneous service personnel. Apart from one of the air-cover aircraft plunging into the sea and exploding (one body was retrieved) the trip was uneventful, and at a point abreast of Durban we detached ourselves and entered Durban harbour. (*Valiant* was destined for repairs in the U.K. after having been advised against a Suez Canal transit). After a short stay at Durban, *Genista* was directed independently to Port Elizabeth, where to my surprise a programme of extensive refit was commenced. The army of workers soon engaged made it necessary to have half the ship's company always on leave, the noise in my quarters became unbearable so I took up residence on shore. It was generally understood that the alterations and additions to the ship were with view to continuance of the war further East, but we were mostly excited about the updating of the asdic and radar installations. One week succeeded another, victory over Europe was announced, Victory celebrations took place in Port Elizabeth with *Genista* as senior officer afloat. The victory thanksgiving service was held at Crusader Ground on the Sunday following the official termination of hostilities with Germany. It was then followed by a service parade under my command. Preceded by ex-servicemen the Naval Detachment consisting of one hundred and fifty-two officers and ratings from the following ships of the Royal Navy: *Genista* .... *Smilex* .... *Marguerite* .... *Rockrose* .... and *Arctic Explorer.* An extract from the

The ship's company leading the naval detachment

local press the day following stated – 'Before a remarkable crowd of 25,000 people the service was most impressive and dramatic, and a vivid touch was lent to the colourful scene by the rows of flags of the Allied Nations that flanked the platform from which the service was conducted'.

Most things have to come to an end, and in due course successful sea trials were completed; with *Marguerite* in company and a multitude of memories striving to compete with 'major war vessels at sea', we commenced the passage, not further east – but to the United Kingdom. In due course I placed *Genista* in the Reserve Fleet at Chatham and was sent on leave awaiting demobilization release in September 1945.

HMS Genista *berthed alongside at Port Elizabeth*

9. Post-War

Demobilization after more than six years of continuous active service was probably the most traumatic thing ever to take place in my life. For those remaining in the Service there would have been dramatic relaxation from the high tension associated with discipline, advancement, weaponry and other such vital things. Others would have looked forward to blessed total retirement from the sordid business of war, and then for thousands like myself we were suddenly of little consequence – except to our dependents.

With a wife and two small children, a demob. suit and £124 war bonus, I managed as best I could to don the mantle of practising parenthood with all its mundane little tasks like shopping, dish-washing, child-minding and a tendency towards low level domestic chatter. By some standards I succeeded well enough in this changing role, but as the months of the resettlement leave went by I found myself becoming dissatisfied with the progress along the path of rehabilitation, particularly in connection with my efforts to retrieve my pre-war knowledge of the curriculum necessary to pass the examination for the master (foreign going) certificate. During these days of de-orientation of naval thinking, I was in regular touch with my old company – British Tanker Co. Ltd., which was anxious to know my likely date for resuming service afloat with their fleet. Frankly this prospect did not give me much joy and had a decent shore job presented itself I would have grabbed it with both hands – but living in the South West of England was not the best place for these opportunities.

And so, after having to return to the first principles of the syllabus prescribed by the Board of Trade regulations, I struggled through the examination for master and was exceedingly relieved to pass – the certificate being signed by the deputy secretary of the Ministry of War Transport on 19th June 1946.

Before the war at sea, it was generally accepted that if one failed to obtain the master's F.G. certificate whilst still unmarried, the chances of doing so after acquiring a family were extremely slim – purely through the economics. These thoughts were frequently on my mind during those months following demobilization, and it can be appreciated how relieved I was to finally succeed. (Nowadays one is paid during the time spent studying ashore for the Ministry of Transport examinations).

Preparation for returning to sea was now the order of things, my old company the British Tanker Co. Ltd. advised me that an appointment as chief officer would be notified in the near future. On 20th July 1946 I joined the mv *British Glory* at Falmouth, sailing soon afterwards for Trinidad in the West Indies to load a cargo for Portland.

On our return to England the ship's arrival was met not only by port officials, but also my wife standing anxiously on the wharf. Little did she realize how completely the chief officer's attention was claimed with cargo work, stores, documents, crew change and invariably the presence of a marine superintendent hovering around like a nasty smell. Needless to say a proper reunion with the wife was out of the question, and her visit was unfortunately somewhat abortive. It was further aggravated on this occasion by a shortfall of cargo, and the 'super' magnanimously excusing me on the grounds of inexperience. Within a bare two days we sailed at 6am bound for the Persian Gulf. My wife was most upset and with a veiled threat had said goodbye very close to tears. Ever since the advent of commercial shipping the shipowner looked upon time spent in port as a dead loss, and the bare minimum of regard paid to the feelings of those on board, other than that he is obliged to conform to through legislation.

On reaching Port Said where we moored in the outer harbour for shipping the canal search-light, one of the port officials arrived on board complaining he had been drenched with water shooting out of the ship's side. An investigation showed a rivet was missing, and a further check explained where the sixty ton shortfall of cargo went!

This was my first experience as chief officer, a responsibility not too unlike that of first lieutenant in a naval vessel – practically all problems outside of the engine-room being his concern. There was much for me to learn, especially in connection with our purpose of the carriage of petroleum cargoes and, looking back I think it was the cargo work which became my chief headache. Years later when my association with the Kent Oil Refinery brought me in close contact with tanker officers, I discovered the mate's main worries seemed to be in connection with deadweight, trim, distribution, tank cleaning and all the rules concerning oil spillage in navigable waters.

Eventually we were in the Gulf again, my first visit in nine years but the smell was the same. I suppose it had something to do with the crude oil and the prevailing north'ly wind as one headed up toward the Shatt al Arab lightship. Whatever it was, its own special pungency was never to be forgotten. We loaded a cargo for Oslo, from where everybody expected the ship to proceed to some U.K. port to change crews and store up. It was not to be however. Whilst the ship was still discharging, the master received instructions to proceed direct to the Persian Gulf on completion of discharge. It was the month of November and needless to say the crew had been planning Christmas at home with their families, so the question was – when should the crew be informed ? At this stage only the chief engineer and myself had been informed. For fear of some jumping ship, the master decided the news should not be broken until the ship was at sea.

Whether informing the crew whilst we were still in port would have prevented subsequent events nobody will ever know for sure, but what actually took place a few days after sailing was best described in the *Daily Mail* headlines of 4th November 1946 – **"Crew fling kettles, pots, pans overboard – Angry tanker men on Persia voyage"**.

It happened during the middle watch when we were half way down the English Channel. The culprits made a very thorough job of it, even the galley stove tops were removed and thrown overboard, to say nothing of the cook's knives and cleavers. The calamity was discovered at the beginning of the morning watch, when the news was brought to me on the bridge. After the sorry inspection the master decided to alter course for Falmouth, and for a while I suppose many of the crew felt satisfied with their perpetration – but not for long, after much talk in the captain's cabin among the department heads it was agreed makeshift improvisation could be carried out to take us as far as Gibraltar. Previous wireless messages were cancelled and any glee among the crew was turned to frustrated disappointment. In due course we anchored off Gibraltar harbour and, inwardly unwilling, I accompanied the master ashore for the purpose of hopefully obtaining the replacement to our galley from the local naval stores. Also, with the crew's behaviour still rankling the master intended to somehow lodge a formal protest. It was never clear to me what actually took place during the period ashore, except for the main business of obtaining the necessary items for the galley. With that completed I returned on board alone. Later, with the master safely back on board we 'hove up' and carried on with the passage through the Mediterranean (and the unknown mutineers? – Perhaps it was the 'least said soonest mended').

This incident only strengthened my resolve to leave the tanker life, even to joining another type of shipping company, but of course my sights were really set on the Trinity House pilotage. So, with the arrival of mail some time later there came from an old war time friend a letter enclosing an application advertisement inserted by the Secretary of the Trinity House pilotage service (the friend was Lieutenant Charles Irving, RNVR, an ex-skipper of convoy escort armed trawlers – a link with former days of anti-submarine warfare training). Rarely did Trinity House 'open the lists,' as it was referred to, so the communication from Charles could not have come at a more appropriate time, and no time was lost with the application rigmarole.

Our next cargo was once again for the Baltic area, this time for Malmö and Stockholm, where we arrived about the festive season with the freezing temperatures and the ice-breakers in the early stages of their activities. We managed to get away from the last port without too much trouble, but rather unwisely commenced the tank cleaning whilst still in the Skagerrak. The canvas hose lines were freezing to the decks and tank coamings, water service piping was bursting and, the crew very uncooperative in the severe cold and wet conditions prevailing at the time. Somewhere in the North Sea the tank washing was suspended due to an effective equipment failure – all hoses were torn to ineffectuality. The ship was bound for Falmouth for drydocking, but with 'dirty' tanks this was out of the question. As chief officer I carried the brunt of this calamitious situation, and as with others on board was apprehensive of our reception at Falmouth Roads, It was still the same marine superintendent who purposefully stepped aboard – although short in stature, John Nesbitt wielded a powerful verbal punch, and what transpired during the thirty minutes in the captain's quarters one could only guess. The outcome of it all was we shipped new and up to date gear and were ordered back to the south-western approaches, where we were to stooge around until the tanks were properly cleaned and in a fit state for the ship to be received by the dry-dock company in Falmouth. I thought the day would never come! Having previously requested leave on special domestic grounds my relief took over after the ship finally settled on the blocks – I was never so relieved to be leaving a ship.

ss *Empire Cedric*

Needless to say I spent very little time at my home before making my way to London, where I chose a small shipping company whose trade was between the United Kingdom and the Continent. The frequent passages across the North Sea and trips in and out the Thames Estuary was exactly what was necessary to prepare me for the much hoped for selection by Trinity House. My resignation was never formally acknowledged by my old company, and it was not without some pangs of conscience that I severed connection with the firm that trained me as an officer, employed me at the closing stages of a time of depression, credited the Provident Fund with the difference between sub.lieutenant's pay and that of second officer and at the end of hostilities give me five years seniority as chief officer with the promise of a command within eighteen months. However, the pull towards my family and ambition was strong and I joined the ss *Empire Cedric* as chief officer on 4th March 1947 at Tilbury Docks.

It was at this time that my wife and I purchased a house at Gravesend, handy to the Tilbury terminal which was close enough to allow me at least one night at home each week. The *Cedric*, like the other two ships in the company were ex LST's, and were operated by one Colonel Bustard under the title F.T. Bustard & Sons Ltd., but later changed to The Continental Line. The trade was the carriage of War Department equipment for the Army of Occupation in Germany, I found it very interesting – a complete contrast from oil, and I soon settled down to the periodic gales, fogs and sometimes the bitterly cold Northerly winds. Hamburg was the main terminal, but occasionally there would be a special cargo for Antwerp.

This new experience was also a testing time, from which I undoubtedly benefitted. Apart from the constant intense interest of the ship's activities, there were moments of excitement too. Upper deck freight was sometimes liable to carry away its lashings – especially unusual items like mobile cranes. Unlike the later purpose built roll-on-roll-off vessels which load through the stern, the LST loaded a vast variety of vehicles through bow doors, and the minimum conversion from their invasion landing days was probably the first commercial venture into the Ro-Ro era. Inherent with the ship's construction, the distribution of cargo often presented unusual stability situations, and in a beam sea she would tend to roll heavily.

Hamburg terminal during the summer of 1947

During my time with the Bustard fleet trade was within the limits of the Elbe and Brest, although subsequently a service was started between Preston and Ireland.

Trinity House pilots were engaged within the limits of the London District pilotage area, together with tugs and mud pilot for the Tilbury Dock. As a result I became acquainted with many of the Pilots, which gave me a good insight into their working conditions.

ss *Empire Baltic*

On the 4th November 1947 I was appointed master of the ss *Empire Baltic**. I would have liked to prolong the subdued feelings of importance and responsibility which comes with command and, although anxious to become a ship's pilot, I remember quite clearly the feeling of indecision when a week before Christmas I was offered the pilotage at Sheerness, there and then, or the North Channel at some later date. Maybe the freezing over that winter of parts of the North Sea, together with an incident in the River Elbe with the German pilot aboard, all helped me to decide. I accepted the Medway position, which as time went on proved the right step to have taken.

From tanks to tractors: the LST of war as a vehicle ferry-ship of commerce

---

* Shortly prior to taking command of the Empire Baltic, *she was suitably fitted with railway lines for the loading of sixteen locomotives, these together with twenty-two heavy road vehicles were taken to Split in Yugoslavia*

10. Trinity House Pilotage

Having clewed up my association with Bustards, the first task after resignation was once again to reorientate my thinking, not only in relation to shipping but, also my mode of living. The shipping master at Tilbury had written the words, "Cessation of sea-going service at own request", in my discharge book, words of sobering finality which continued to cross my mind during the months ahead as I diligently absorbed the unrecorded priceless words of wisdom, the tutoring pilots, sometimes sparingly imparted. Would I ever learn all they knew?

Fortunately we had managed to hang on to our Morris 8 throughout the war. New cars were unobtainable and second-hand ones cost the earth. So with my home and family in Gravesend it became invaluable for travelling to the pilot station at Sheerness at any time of the day or night. A set minimum number of trips had to be performed with licensed pilots, and for our own obvious benefit we endeavoured to perform as many as possible. We very soon discovered how completely true was the quotation: "Repetition is the essence of piloting". I keep using the word "we" because two weeks before I presented myself at Sheerness to commence the three months' probationary period, another ex RNR candidate for a licence had started his 'tripping', Gordon Taylor was therefore two weeks senior to myself. Like the Navy, seniority was quite important in all things connected with Trinity House.

Money was a little scarce in those days, the travelling expenses to reach a ship and return to our homes or the pilot station on completion of the act of pilotage came from our own pockets. The wearing of uniforms with black buttons had not at that time been introduced and the wear and tear on our civilian clothes became a further expense. My demob' suit became very useful for work at night, bad weather or climbing aboard dirty colliers. At that time in Sheerness the war-time Blackburn Seamen's Hostel was still functioning; situated close to the railway station it became our home from home. Ideally suiting our modest needs, the food was excellent and accommodation clean and adequate at the charge of half a crown per night.

It became obvious fairly soon that each of the five Medway pilots, George Butters, Bob Manson, Jack Hannan, Fred Seargent and Roy Milne, had their particular ways, noticeably so in connection with their application to the actual acts of pilotage; I refer mainly to pilotage within the River Medway and East & West Swale waterway, which tree or stump that would be religiously used by one, would have no place in another pilot's store of local knowledge. This I soon discovered very confusing, and together with their personal idiosyncrasies made the business of formulating my own method strangely interesting. Needless to say some pilots became more favoured for doing trips with than others, with the consequences that can be imagined. Reflecting back, they were interesting characters (maybe as I became) of whom alone one could write a book. One I remember was noted for his complete absence of any words of amplifying advice, while another was prone to assume the candidate sufficiently capable to take over – with disastrous results on more than one occasion. There were tricks of the trade to be gleaned from each of these pilots, and our task was to assemble together a suitable and workable method in order to acquire the expertise and knowledge upon which we had set our sights.

East & West Swale
The district for which I was hoping to be licensed embraced the East and West Swale (the water separating the Isle of Sheppey from the mainland of the N.E. Kent coast), River Medway below the Rochester Bridge, and out through all the channels northward to the Sunk Light Vessel (off Harwich), eastward through all channels of the Thames Estuary, the waters and channels around the Goodwin Sands, and together with the Dover Straits to Dungeness in the English Channel.

The curriculum was daunting, but we persevered over our respective sets of charts, criss-crossed with pencil lines of courses and innumerable bearings with distances. Facilities for chartwork at the pilot station were poor, so most of the study and work was done at home. With the family around they were difficult times to learn and memorize some three hundred buoy characteristics, together with hundreds of courses, bearings, distances, lightships, beacons and fog signals. Then there was the actual art of shiphandling and local knowledge – there were times when it seemed just beyond capability.

I can quite remember the day I presented myself at Trinity House in London, and the Elder Brother before whom I stood nervously waiting for the first question. With thirty-six years gone by I still remember it. "Describe the rate and flow of the tide at the northeast Spit Buoy". Easy to ask such questions with all the relevant charts spread out before him, but I had the correct answer transposed to the

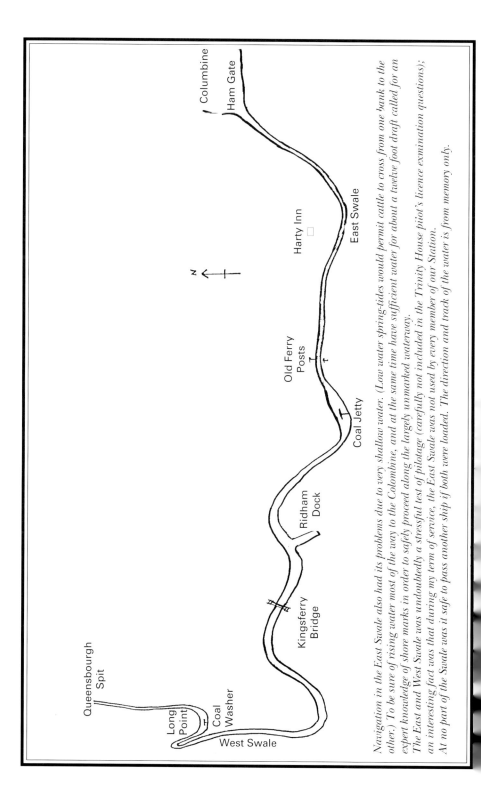

Queensbourgh Spit

Long Point

Coal Washer

West Swale

Kingsferry Bridge

Ridham Dock

Coal Jetty

Old Ferry Posts

Harty Inn

East Swale

Ham Gate

Columbine

N

Navigation in the East Swale also had its problems due to very shallow water. (Low water spring-tides would permit cattle to cross from one bank to the other.) To be sure of rising water most of the way to the Columbine, and at the same time have sufficient water for about a twelve foot draft called for an expert knowledge of shore marks in order to safely proceed along the largely unmarked waterway.

The East and West Swale was undoubtedly a stressful test of pilotage (carefully not included in the Trinity House pilot's licence exmination questions); an interesting fact was that during my term of service, the East Swale was not used by every member of our Station.

At no part of the Swale was it safe to pass another ship if both were loaded. The direction and track of the water is from memory only.

time of high water Sheerness – for which it took a couple of minutes for him to verify. This may have given me the confidence I needed because after a thorough analysis of the estuary channels this autocratic mariner shook hands with me and said my licence would be sent on in due course.

Having been found a fit and competent person to act as a pilot for the purpose of conducting ships from Rochester Bridge to the Nore and vice versa – also from the Nore to the Sea via the North and South Channels, I wasted no time before becoming gainfully employed; our supply of money had been sorely depleted. Soon after becoming a pilot we were fortunate to purchase a suitable house on the Isle of Sheppey. Also at that time my mother passed away at Gravesend. It was a great shock. Arrangements were made for her to be buried with my father in South Wales. Needless to say there was much turmoil at that time; shipping was on the increase and settling in to the new house had the customary problems.

Since 1929, or from age of sixteen, about twenty years of my life had been given to deep sea, but now my form of employment was to change somewhat. It was to start learning how to associate with a variety of shore people.

Trinity House Tower Hill

The pilots in my district were in the public eye.This was due to Sheerness being a small town and the pilots were conspicuous being constantly in uniform. A further reason was due to much of our work being connected with shipping in and out of the West Swale, each act necessitating the raising of the Kingsferry Bridge – thus closing the only road access to and from the Isle of Shippey. This was a constant irritation to the locals and added to our notoriety.

As beginners we were compelled to continue the in-depth study of our licensed district, which meant constantly pouring over charts to the point where one developed a photographic-style memory of any particular part of the Thames Estuary. This was a three year slog mostly in our own time and, in preparation for what was termed the 'all draft licence', for which was required a further examination. It was during this three year period that one became proficient and self-confident. It was a wise precaution adopted by the Elder Brethren of Trinity House before permitting a pilot to conduct the largest and deepest ships afloat.

The present day Sheerness Pilot Station, a far cry from the old 'hut'. It is situated on top of the Garrison Po... old fortification, with a commanding view of the Thames Estuary.
The occasion was an official visit to the area by His Royal Highness Prince Philip, behind whom can be se... the senior pilot Captain Howard Greelees and the deputy master of Trinity House.

The Seven Men of the Medway

The laws governing the engaging of a pilot could be confusing to some, consequently it was not uncommon when in doubt to refer directly to the secretary of Trinity House for guidance. Broadly speaking, ships carrying passengers were subject to compulsory pilotage, as were ships bound from or to ports outside the Home Trade limits of the Elbe and Brest. There were exceptions however for small ships which had regularly used the district for longer periods than sixty days. It was quite common for these small regular traders to become involved in differences of opinion over being 'compulsory' or 'exempt', thus involving the pilots, the agents, owners and of course possibly the ultimate authority.

Known in the district as the 'seven men of the Medway', we had an elected leader who performed the duties of chairman, spokesman and secretary. Being strictly self-employed people this onerous task was largely a thankless one, but essential to our gainful survival – as mentioned before, the shipowner was a hard person to deal with.

As time went on, together with my compatriot we started to take stock of the pilot station and its method of function. The actual structure was primitive to say the least, what appeared to be the only claim to advancement being the telephone. Fresh from service afloat we considered an updating of the station as a whole should be started. Change however is not always welcome; we were the subject of much criticism together with comments bordering on threats – but we persevered. Just as I am interested today in the tremendous improvements and changes which have come about in all aspects of the shipping industry, likewise I feel the operators of today would be interested to know how our pilot station in the Medway functioned and looked like during the years immediately following the 39-45 war. We referred to our station or lookout as the "Hut", which was exactly what it was – a low almost flat roofed wooden single spaced structure, very similar to the type of railway shed seen alongside the track; in fact its main members were railway sleepers. Wholly coated with a black bitumen paint, this edifice nestled in the lee of the Garrison Point seaward parapet and, from its end window we had a commanding view of the Swatchway and Little Nore, out along the Medway approach channel and Great Nore – to as far as the Redsand Towers and beyond in clear weather. The lookout position was probably its sole redeeming feature. There was no running water – that had to be carried; heating was by way of a type of pot belly stove, the source of supply of coal for it was something I never fully understood! There was always a cat, without which we would have not slept soundly when on night time turn pilot duty. The Pied Piper of Hamlin would have had a field-day! Apart from two iron cots, there was an old ship's cabin compactum for washing face and hands, a sloping lift-up desk near the telephone and, six very old wooden square lockers, which I believe originated in the Sheerness Royal Dockyard, having at some earlier time been used as seaman's lockers aboard naval vessels.

The earthwork upon which the hut was placed was about ten feet above the approach walkway and in order to save time a painter's ladder was propped against the wall under the hut. How somebody never managed to break his neck will remain a mystery. The other useful purpose the ladder served was in connection with the fact we had no toilet! Fortunately however there was one a few yards from the foot of the ladder belonging to the local Army and our senior pilot being on friendly terms with their mess, we kept a key on permanent loan. We had two pilot boats which were operated by two thoroughly experienced watermen; this number was increased to three not too long after we had appeared on the scene. The boats themselves, of open build from witch elm, were prone to giving trouble, mostly engine, but the hulls themselves were past their prime. In those days it was common for ships to circle around flying the G flag or blowing frantically for the pilot boat whilst the boatman sweated to start the engine. I draw this picture to explain the dire need for complete up-dating of the Medway pilot station. Apart from the location, there seemed to be nothing that was not in need of operational improvement.

Gordon Taylor and I were not completely alone with these ideas, as time went on two more new pilots were made and support was beginning to come from some of the more senior men. Application was made to the Trinity House for the levying of a boarding and landing charge against the shipowner. At the same time we set about framing a set of bye-laws appertaining to our station which we hoped would be approved by the various authorities. Up until this time each pilot contributed an agreed sum of money each month into a pool, from which the entire establishment running costs were drawn. Frequently this pool would run dry and we were all called upon for a further donation of cash. These contributions increased with the continued deterioration of the boats. The under-draft men, although earning considerably less money than the all-draft pilots, were called upon to subscribe equal sums. Not only were we self-employed people – that which we earned from the shipowner we kept – but the work was divided on a cut-throat system. There were no less than five rosters, each pilot taking his turn in strict rotation, thus producing the anomaly of upper-draft pilots performing more acts of pilotage than the under-draft men. As new pilots we were not going to be too popular bringing about the necessary changes.

Medway Pilots Association

After rearranging the rosters in order to ensure each pilot performed the same number of acts of pilotage, discussion was started for the formation of an association with limited liability. At the same time plans were made for the construction of a new pilot station as our numbers were gradually being increased to cope with the increasing trade of the Medway. The Corporation of Trinity House, recognizing the future development of the Isle of Grain by the British Petroleum Co, and its certain effect on the pilot service for the Medway district, set about discussion covering the whole spectrum. We were invited to compile draft by-laws, a task which Taylor and myself gladly tackled. Much help was received from the secretary of Trinity House in the formation of what became the Medway Pilots Association Limited, its articles of association covering the newly constructed pilot station, the new pilot boat with its legal ownership and operation plus other important aspects concerning an efficient and business-like service to the shipping industry. This reformation by a comparatively small

The first pilot boat we had built when starting the replacement programme. She was identical to the craft used by the cutters on station at the Sunk and Dungeness and could stand up to any weather.

band of pilots was taking place at a momentous time insofar as the United Kingdom Pilots' Association was concerned. Criticism of the executive by the delegates was strong at the 1960 conference and, the Medway delegate leading the attack was fortunate to have the support of one or two other stations. It was certainly fortunate that the Medway dealings with the B.P. Tanker Company at this particular time were satisfactory. As the main shipowner our fortunes were linked and we went forward together.

We were not alone in this rapid progress, the local tugowning firm soon placed an order for a more powerful tug. We were happy to be consulted with regard their further building programme – after all who knows better than the pilot what assistance is needed in the handling of large ships. Many of the tug's crew members were personally known to the pilots. In fact the senior tug skipper had previously been employed by the pilots as waterman/coxswain. The tug/pilot relationship was considered first class, something for which we were envied by other pilot stations. With the introduction of VHF night work became possible and so the steady progress of the Medway shipping industry continued. In step with this the shipping agents up and down the river prospered along with hundreds more ancillary workers connected with the refinery, Medway towns port and cargo expansion and not forgetting the planned transition of the Sheerness Royal Dockyard into a commercial cargo handling terminal. Later still it became a main Continental ferry terminal for the roll-on roll-off fast carriers.

Medway Pilot 6, *the latest craft 1968. Pilot Vallings is at the stern.*

Trinity House Pilotage

The years of the 1950s and 60s were without doubt exciting ones in the Medway as we took our bread off the water. With the pilot complement steadily increasing to cope with the increasing volume of shipping, so our cash flow grew, enabling the station to place orders for bigger and better pilots boats – a most vital part of our service.

My lifestyle started to broaden somewhat after the first year or so of pilotage. The tension and nervousness common to beginners of ship handling gradually diminished, although there is the odd unfortunate pilot who seemed to retain the stomach wobble feelings for longer periods. Trinity House were well aware of this and their rules stipulated a minimum of seven years' experience before becoming eligible for selected pilotage – (well established shipping companies like to appoint a particular pilot to handle their ships – sometimes even a second man if their volume of shipping was great enough). Either through envy, or just the post-war general levelling of the business of living, this choice work as it was called became frowned upon by the main body of pilots in the London District, causing much inconvenience and ill-feeling among shipowners and pilots alike.

The tug Kestrel *meeting an inward tanker in the Little Nore. She was the first of ever-increased powerful tugs necessary for the bigger and bigger tankers using the Medway.*

In the Medway during those days of the 'fifties our main gripe was too much work or too few pilots whichever way one looked at it. However, it certainly tended to increase our ship-handling expertise. Later, when ships were approaching the hundred thousand ton mark and, given the choice of a big or small ship, I would invariably select the large one as a sort of challenge to my capabilities. Although the pilotage fee varied with the size and draft of a vessel, a pilot would receive a fixed sum of money for each act of pilotage. This uniform system of payment for our services was known as the common purse, all our earnings were pooled into a central fund operated by a local firm of accountants, each pilot receiving a set amount based on the number of acts of pilotage each month. The surplus money in the pool was shared among the pilots each quarter pro rata with the number of acts each pilot had performed.

Returning home on Danish ship Margareta *from the cruising stations at the Sunk and Dungeness. I am at extreme right beside Captain Horsley M.C.*

Joining the Clubs

In spite of the pressure of work and claims on my domestic obligations, which included my two school-age children, I somehow managed to accept the invitation to join the newly formed Royal Naval Reserve Officers London Club. After the first couple of monthly meetings held at the RNVR Club in Hill Street the venue was changed to the Naval & Military Club, Piccadilly. Soon afterwards the founder president, Commodore Robinson, left for the antipodes after handing over to Captain G.C.H. Noakes, RNR, Elder Brother of Trinity House. All this was taking place in the mid-fifties. Brimming with ambition I was grateful to accept from Robie, before his departure, his offer to propose my name for membership of the Honourable Company of Master Mariners.

Looking back, those days for me were pretty momentous. In 1948 Trinity House granted me a licence to pilot ships and, at about the same time I was awarded the Royal Naval Reserve Decoration. I

With my sister house at Strensham Hill

became involved in the early formation days of the RNR Officers' Club,
serving on committee and in due
course on list of vice-presidents. I came
to the conclusion years ago that those
were the years when the responsibilities of the home and family were under strain. Not satisfied with joining
the local golf club and becoming a
keen player, I suffered the initiation
of Freemasonry, becoming a member
of the Isle Of Sheppey Lodge No.6769.
Not content with being a silent member of our association I attended pilotage meetings and conferences, also
a stint as officer in charge of the pilot
cutters. The longest unthanked task however was the Medway pilots
tax representative – income tax was a hot chestnut which nobody else
seemed willing to become involved. My job was to keep a check on all
monies paid out to maintain the pilot station, together the individual
pilot's expenditure in the performance of his duties. These outgoings
were assessed as a percentage of our earnings and were under
constant review by the revenue department.

The Honourable Company of Master Marines
These activities took up much of my off duty time, a situation which
as time went by was to take its toll on my domestic life. The objects and
functioning of the Honourable Company of Master Mariners ap-
pealed to me and it was with a feeling of privilege that I served on its
Court of Assistants and Technical Committee. For me the *Wellington*
(the Honourable Company's headquarters ship alongside the Victoria Embankment in London) meant the revival of earlier day friendships and former acquaintances, shipmasters under whom I had
served and one or two renewals of real shipmate friendships. Good
examples would be Captain R.L. Friendship, commodore master B.P.
Tanker Co. He had changed little from our days together as apprentices – cheery and smiling as ever, with never an ill word toward others.
Above all we were proud and satisfied with our achievements, as was
the case with Captain R. Marsh, superintendent of training apprentices, B.P. Tanker Co. Ltd., which was certainly his correct niche in life
and for which with his wide grin he was admirably suited. There were

many others that stood out, including Captain St.Geo. Glasson, ex.commodore, Elder Brother of Trinity House, whom I had stood nervously in front of as an under-draft pilot for breaking one of the unwritten rules of pilotage. (Acting on the advice of my senior fellow pilots I refused to pilot an Everard ship away from Ridham Dock during the dark hours. My explanation was accepted by the Elder Brethren and the salutary lesson typified the characteristics of self-employed pilotage at that time.) The fine qualities of Mr W.T.C. Smith followed by H.M. Disney, MBE with their clerkship of the Honourable Company have been better described by others, so my admiration is of small count.

HMS Wellington *was purchased in 1948 by the Honourable Company and moored at Temple Stairs, retaining her name as our headquarters ship*

I will always remember Captain L.A. Hill, DSC, RD, RNR, whom for a while was chairman of the Technical Committee. He showed much interest in my suggestion that pilots unable to disembark at Dungeness due to bad weather (or any other U.K. cruising pilot cutter station), should proceed to the Lisbon pilot cutter cruising station at the mouth of the Tagus River. Port officials at Lisbon had assured me that the water around the corner from Cape Roca, off Cascais, where the pilot cutter cruised, was invariably smooth, a fact which certainly tallied with my visits to that area. Captain Hill studied my proposal and I still keep in a letter the details he wrote explaining the problems associated with Salazar, the Portuguese dictator, insofar as the liberalization of immigration laws were concerned, and regrettably no further action could be. I still think however that the idea was a good one, both from the safety point of view and present day alternative costs.

The temptation to stray off the main theme is ever present whilst writing these words, so to return. Mention must be made of the Right Reverend Gerald A. Ellison, D.D., Bishop of Chester, the HCMM honorary chaplain at the time of which I write. His last address given at St.Michael's, Cornhill, before becoming Bishop of London, was one never to be forgotten by me on account of two things he said: his association with St.Michael's and the Honourable Company was very particular to himself because his father at one time was Vicar of St.Michael's and he predicted that the day would come when all people would be 'directed' in all their actions. Since that time I have come to believe that the two words **progress** and **freedom** are complete misnomers.

My active connection with the Honourable Company at this time of my career would not be complete without some words on the Technical Committee, which during the time I served on it was fortunate to have very experienced members. This was particularly so in the case of an important suggestion which had been placed before the Company by our member Captain Dennis Bunn, DSC, RNR (North Channel pilot). His contention was that in fog, when two ships were approaching one another, neither should alter course to port if collision was imminent. That was the beginning of long and very informed discussion at our regular meetings over a lengthy period. Few qualified single ship handlers were more entitled to expound on the dangers surrounding that part of the Collision Rules which were in force on 1st September 1965. During poor visibility the Barrow Deep with its end-on traffic was a constant problem to contend with and when two ships were not in sight of each other, those exercising Rule 21 did so (almost) at their peril. Bunn's proposal therefore received my complete support and, after much thrashing of words with the various ministries and others, the International Regulations for Preventing Collisions at Sea were changed to prohibit the alteration of the ship's head to port at the crucial moment when using radar, and when the ships are not in sight of each other. I have among my permanent records a letter from Dennis Bunn in which he graciously extends thanks for the help he received in connection with the 'Port Rule' and, what became known as the "Bunn Fight".

The business of living was very full in those days, with swift changes from work, domestics, nautical interests and even recreation. Slowly the golf bug started to take effect, with the inevitable extra claims on one's spare time. The Trinity House Pilots Golfing Society formation was hailed as a huge success and wetted my appetite for the winter facilities at Estoril in Portugal. With new pilots and their young families there was never any problem exchanging my summer leave. I was very impressed with the sheltered area of water off Cascais and Estoril, which appeared the most perfect station for a cruising pilot cutter.

I hope I will be excused the obsessional views on the Tagus disembarkation area, but before ending the topic it will be of interest to readers maybe to learn of a sequel. During one of my visits to Estoril I had occasion to visit the Lisbon port captain, who during the interview telephoned the British Naval Attaché – I was astounded to learn it was no other than (Midshipman) Westmacott, but now Sir Percy – he was equally astonished. Briefly, he suggested I spoke to the British Consul who was attending a party at the embassy the following day. It turned out to be a woman and, although very interested she confirmed all the obstacles spoken of by others. As for Westmacott, we had a few pleasant words about *Revenge* days, and the memorable trip to Scapa Flow. I came away thinking that my selection of the gun room was pretty good; he had volunteered for submarines and, as commanding officer had greatly distinguished himself.

Flooding of the Thames Estuary
One again it is necessary to go back to an earlier chapter of this transitional business of living, to mention the disastrous affects of the 1953 flooding in our part of the Thames Estuary. It came about as a result of combination of high winds building up water around the south east of England, with finally a sudden shift of these strong winds to the north. With much of Sheppey below sea level the sea-wall protection was inadequate to stop the swollen estuary surging across the low lying parts of the Isle of Sheppey. The Royal Dockyard suffered badly, with one submarine rolled over to her side in one of the drydocks. Ridham Dock in the west Swale suffered severe damage through pressure of water, causing the dock wall to collapse, taking cranes and railway rolling stock down into the gaping cracks. The Kent Oil Refinery installations were put out of action for several weeks (this was the year when the refinery had started to refine crude oil). Rochester was affected too, with serious dislocation to wharf opera-

tions and mooring facilities. The commercial shipping side of the Medway almost came to a stop. Our normal workload of thirty-odd acts of pilotage per pilot fell to five ships for the thirty days following the disaster – the receipts did not cover expenses.

RNR Training

It was probably the enforced slackening of shipping activity as a result of the flood that focused my thoughts towards RNR training. In normal times the pilots on the Medway were very busy and time away from the station performing training was not exactly welcomed by the body. Nevertheless an annual system of rest periods was accepted, each pilot receiving fourteen days absence from work, with the detailed list submitted to the superintendent of pilots at Gravesend. Due to applications for long periods of absence from civil duties to perform 'training' not being approved', the Admiralty promulgated (A.C.R. 113/6/51) in a letter dated 10th April 1951:-

> R.N.R. OFFICERS IN PILOTAGE SERVICE
>
> As you know, the Trinity House authority are unable to grant you special leave to undergo peace-time obligatory training, but having nevertheless undertaken to release you for mobilised service if required, as soon as you can be spared from your pilotage duties. It has therefore been decided to retain you on List 1 of the RNR until you become liable for removal from the List or transfer to the Retired List, in accordance with current regulations.
>
> 2. Commanders RNR have no peace-time training at present and so are not liable for removal from the Active List under Article 137. Lieutenant Commanders RNR have to undergo 28 days triennially and become liable for removal from the Active List or transfer to the Retired List if they fail to fulfil their training obligations within 6 years of 1st November 1950.
>
> 3. Officers who render themselves liable for removal from the Active List, may be invited to transfer to List 11, if eligible and considered suitable.
>
> 4. In view of the difficulties which RNR officers employed by Trinity House may experience with regard to the fulfilment of their training obligations, Admiral Commanding Reserves is prepared to consider applications to undergo training in two period of about 14 days each (instead of a continuous 28 days) on the clear understanding that no officer will be accepted for a part of a course, for which there is a limited number of vacancies, if another officer who can complete the full course would otherwise be deprived of a place on the course. If you wish to carry out training in broken periods in this way, you should give as much notice as possible but at the same time you must accept the fact that your application will have to be refused, if all vacancies for the full course are filled within 14 days of the commencement of the course.
>
> Signed - A.C.R.

An application in the last quarter of 1952 to perform training was accepted, but not approved by Trinity House. A letter was written addressed to the Medway delegate to the United Kingdom Pilots' Association, with copies to Trinity House, Registrar General of Shipping & Seamen and, the Superintendents of Trinity House pilots at Gravesend, Dover and Harwich. The eight paragraph letter set out the details concerning two previous applications for training which had been cancelled through non-approval from my Authority and, it was hoped a satisfactory solution arrived at. No reply was received from any of the recipients, I did however get an acknowledgement on Customs and Excise note paper (negative reference) and, dated at Chatham 30th October 1952.

> "Dear Sir,
> With reference to your letter of 28th October 1952 regarding naval training, I have had a telephone conversation with the Principal on the matter. He states, quoting a minute 7652 of 24th November 1950, that it is contrary to Trinity House policy to allow pilots leave for the purpose of attending training. I have accordingly to inform you that leave for that purpose cannot be allowed.
> Yours faithfully
>
> T.G. Radford Esq.
> Sheerness   Superintendent

Questionable as it may appear and, with the facts known to my station colleagues but not their unanimous approval, with seven days leave due me I accepted inclusion in the senior officers' tactical course at Londonderry. From 29th November to 9th December 1952 we were absorbed on the floor with the 'convoy games' at HMS *Sea Eagle*, the Commanding Officer Northern Ireland received a signal from the Admiralty stated that Lieutenant Commander Radford would return to his place of civil employment on completion of the course! I returned to face the pique of our principal and respond to the inevitable censure, but little did I realize then that the expected verdict was to be followed two or three years later by malevolence.

A bitter disappointment

With my close association with nautical activities in London, particularly by way of service on committees, my list of acquaintances grew. One such person, a Naval Commander was privileged to serve on the RNR Advisory Committee. He also sat with myself on the Royal Naval Reserve Officers' (London) Club and, on an occasion in London during the mid-fifties shattered my ambition. He felt obliged to tell me how my name had in the ordinary way come up before the board for promotion on List I to Commander RNR and, how the routine contact with the employer had been made by a telephone call to Trinity House. The reply it appeared was made by the principal, to the effect that Mr Radford was not amenable to discipline. The bitter disappointment of being passed over remained with me for many years. Now in my declining years it is to be hoped that certain people felt some twinges of remorse before leaving this world; their departure roughly coincided with the time I surrendered my licence.

By the time the end of the fifties was approaching, great changes and improvements had come about in the Medway. The pilot strength had increased to over two dozen, with efficient pilot cutters and crews. A port information and lookout centre was established on Garrison Point which came under the Medway Conservancy Board. The Medway approach channel had been deepened and the old Class I mooring buoys in the Sheerness harbour removed. The North and South Kent lighted buoys had been established deep into the harbour at the point of north/south turn. The local tugs had been increased in size and efficiency and the pilot/tug relationship second to none. The VHF now becoming widely used, enabled the night handling of loaded tankers outwards – the port was becoming an important tanker terminal.

A Tragedy

Sobering thoughts are statistics which show that one day in three in the Thames Estuary much of the time the visibility would be below one thousand yards. Over a million tons of shipping per day passes Southend on average in the course of a year. There are numerous spots in the channels of the Thames Estuary where a ship drawing 35 feet would not float at half tide, causing much anxiety for the ship handler when the visibility was uncertain; could he reach the next 'hole' before it shut in completely or, would the 'bed' be already occupied by the time he reached there! During my first few years the North Edinburgh Channel was marked with blind buoys, the deep water being found in the South Edinburgh Channel which had the lighted buoys. Of about the period I am writing now it had reversed, with the deep water in the North Edinburgh and having lighted buoys, and the South Edinburgh having silted up considerably. Only those people who have handled a fully loaded ship drawing thirty odd feet rounding the North East Shingles buoy at about half ebb tide, will know what it feels like with visibility down to a thousand yards. This work took its toll on pilot's health and lives. It brings to my mind the terrible disaster in the Knob Channel with the sinking of the *Truculent*. The small coasting tanker *Devina* with channel pilot Captain Davies on board was bound for the Sunk Pilot Station on this particular dark night. Coming down from the Mid Barrow bound for the Medway was HM submarine *Truculent* in the hands of her commanding officer. On a clear night in the vicinity of the spot where these two vessels collided, it would be possible to see at least two dozen buoys flashing within a two mile radius, making identification sometimes difficult. The *Truculent* sank quickly with only three subsequent survivors in spite of tremendous efforts made by surface rescue vessels – mostly Medway participation. Captain Davies never properly recovered from the tragedy and died within two years.

Radar

As the advent of the sixties approached, radar was raising its ugly head and, armchair navigators by the dozen were either busying themselves advocating the wonderful worth of the radar, or telling us how to use it. *Lloyd's Shipping Gazette* (with temerity according to some) published some words of mine advising caution with the reliance on radar. In large letters they headed my views "RADAR A HAZARD"! With its rapid introduction to practically all ships, with the steady improvements to the sets themselves, I, like many more had my share of groping along the routes and channels of the pilotage district. To my mind the situation has changed little; admittedly the *Crystal Jewel/ British Aviator* instances (a tragic collision case) have become less frequent as a result of simulated training and application. But I question the worth for passage expedition and, that includes the

normal high speeds of present day shipping – it is the consumer who pays. The exponents of the high pressure tech' system are quick to point out the hopelessness of attempting to anchor the very large carriers afloat today when in reduced visibility. So they keep going, to satisfy the serpent greed.

On board ss British Sailor *(32,000 tonnes)*

74

Old acquaintances

Little did I think when I resigned from the British Tanker Co. in 1947, that the day would come when I would be seeing and handling ships of their fleet almost daily. Equally remote was the thought of hearing frequent little snatches of the people I had known or sailed with – even to meeting some again. Of Captain Thorburn, there was the sad story of the war days, when pulling away from his torpedoed ship which was ablaze, he subsequently earned the displeasure of his superiors for not returning through the flaming oil to rescue crew seen to be left on board. Another, a certain chief engineer who never failed to see or send word to me on the bridge if by chance I was piloting his particular ship – we picked him and other survivors up off the west coast of Africa in 1943 when I was first lieutenant of *Aubretia*. Then there was Captain Mott, who had served his time in sail; he was chief officer of the *British Empress* when I was a third year apprentice on board. He was known for being very brusque and tough. The day I stepped on board his bridge to pilot and berth the super tanker he commanded, he was momentarily speechless to my greeting. Recovering himself he said, "Well I suppose you can do the job", and left me to it. There were others like Midshipman Vance, whom I learned parted company with the Royal Navy, to become an uncertificated third mate. He was torpedoed and earned due recognition for outstanding command of his lifeboat-full of survivors. Then during the 'fifties' I bumped into Midshipman Scott at a function in London, he was a Lieutenant Commander and had just completed some outstanding peacetime feat in command of a submarine crossing the western ocean submerged.

It would be remiss of me not to mention my old friend and shipmate Captain Ron Marsh, whom I saw most of on board the *Wellington*. He swallowed the anchor in 1938 to secure an appointment with one of the ministries. With the advent of war he joined the R.A.F. specializing in navigation. He became the chief examiner at the R.S.A.A.F. 42nd. Air School in Port Elizabeth. (We literally bumped into each other parking our cars in the same street during 1945.) After our demobilization he was fortunate to be appointed superintendent training of apprentices with our old employer the British Tanker Company; a more suitable person it would have been difficult to find. We enjoyed the frequent times we met on board the *Wellington* – it was a loss when he died before his time.

One last acquaintance I must mention that will tickle some readers, a man from Wales who was the chief steward whilst I served as the third mate. At that time the company rewarded the chief stewards with a bonus if a surplus of stores remained on completion of the voyage. Our chief officer in this particular ship was a Mr Caws, who liked to retire regularly after lunch to the lavatory with his magazine. Three feet across the alleyway was the chief steward's cabin door, from where he maintained a vigil because an inordinate amount of toilet paper was being used. It seems that on one of Mr Caws' lengthy visits, the wincing strain on the Welshman as he listened to each piece of paper being torn off was too great. Emerging from the lavatory Caws was confronted by the steward, who complained bitterly of excessive use of toilet paper, to which the chief officer replied; "Rubbish – I only use three pieces, one up, one down, and a polish".

It was about this period of my Trinity House days that yet another memorable friend reappeared: Lieutenant Ken Dimbleby, RSAVR, with his charming wife visited London. Their home was in South Africa, Ken's father being the Editor of the *Eastern Province Herald* newspaper in Port Elizabeth. At the time I first met Ken, he was the port liaison officer at Durban when I arrived there in *Genista* escorting the lame duck battleship HMS *Valiant*. We became great friends and it was wonderful to see them again. Included in their full programme was a visit to Richard Dimbleby the famous B.B.C. announcer and relative. Ken was seeking a publisher for his new book *The Night The Rains Came*. I read the manuscript and thought the 'immorality law' plot a good one and made good reading, but I never discovered whether it was every published – I did however some years later see a play on T.V. which was very similar. Ken's first book was called *Hostilities Only*, based on his survival after the sinking of the cruiser *Cornwall* when he was a bell bottom. The autographed copy he gave me was loaned to somebody and never returned – a small sad thing in my life. Subsequently, as my domestic life became somewhat tangled, we seemed to stop writing to each other, which is regrettable. Through the Dimblebys I met several other South African people during those days when their forces were helping and participating in our winning the war. They were people on both sides of the political fence and it is a tragedy that now in the 80's their country is so torn apart.

Royal Dockyard Closure
Returning to the life on the Medway, in their wisdom the Admiralty and Government decided to close the Sheerness Royal Dockyard. Originally a rumour, reality came with the transfer to Chatham of

personnel and the pensioning off of older servants. The centuries old connection with the Royal Navy was a difficult knot to untie for many of the people living on the Isle of Sheppey and grave were the doubts that the usurping commercial venture would become a success as an alternative form of revenue. Slowly however the new operations in the port of Sheerness became firmly established. It would have been a brave prediction at that time to visualize the port becoming a prominent continental ferry terminal, or that the harbour-owned limits would include the construction of an exporting steel making plant and modern facilities for the handling of large roll-on-roll-off vessels. However, of the time reached in this narrative, the Kent Oil Refinery was reaching its peak throughput of oil. The seven large-ship jetties were constantly occupied, with a regular supply of ballast and loaded ships awaiting berths at anchor in the Great Nore and Warps. Shipping by pilot cutter was not practicable and the pilot was obliged to do so by tug, a very acceptable arrangement, particularly during a weather tide with easterly wind, when ships lying to an anchor produce little or no lee side.

By this time additional pilots had been made, with the result that the average age had dropped considerably. Although very sound and qualified, the new men's expertise and knowledge of pilots politics

The Danish freighter Leica Maersk *passing through the old Kingsferry Bridge (just prior to demolition). The London based* Gazalee *tug would have a slack rope only, its function primarily being to assist the docking and undocking at Ridham Dock also with the difficult negotiation of the near 180 degree bend in the channel approaching Queenborough known as Long Point*

did not equal their seniors, with the result that sometimes the decisions, made in true democratic fashion, were not always the wisest. Our business of maintaining an efficient pilot station produced numerous problems, some of which were real hot potatoes; such a one was Selected Pilotage. A widely held view, which I share, is that familiarity with a particular operation tends to enhance results, in this case reducing the risks associated with spasmodic application. How therefore can one blame the shipowner for requiring the regular services of a senior pilot! Democracy however has its price, with conformity sometimes akin to the walking of a tight-rope.

Milford Haven

It was during this expansionist period that the controllers started looking at the possibilities of Milford Haven as a terminal for large tankers. Captain Noakes was chairman of the Pilotage Committee at the time. He selected three pilots from Falmouth, Southampton and Medway to accompany himself and Secretary Rawling-Smith on a visit to Milford.It was interesting studying the local waters and the discussions with resident mariners on the aspects of handling large tankers in the Haven. I was elated at being the Medway pilot selected, but more to the point was the thought running through my mind that it would be wonderful if I could transfer to Milford Haven as a working pilot – after all I was born in South Wales and had spent my boyhood not far away in Narbeth.

The circumstances of my being passed over for a brass hat still rankled, so that I had no qualms in voicing my thoughts to the secretary. Eventually the preliminaries were completed and a decision made to select three senior pilots for transfer to Milford. The letter from Trinity House inviting me to apply for this transfer duly arrived, but my excitement was short lived by my wife's refusal to entertain the idea of moving to Pembrokeshire – it was a bitter disappointment. Not for the first time, an opportunity to put behind me that side of my work I found thoroughly unpleasant was to slip through my hands. I refer to the interminable periods we down pilots were obliged to spend on the cruising cutters at the Sunk and Dungeness, just waiting to get off and start the tedious journey home. (Earlier, an appointment with the Crown Agents as marine officer in the Gilbert & Ellis Islands was subject to my wife accompanying me, but a life in the Pacific Islands did not appeal to her – unfortunately for me). It was with particular regret that I was obliged to decline the prospects of transferring to Milford Haven. So I tried to resign myself

Dierdre, the air hostess

to the situation that prevailed at the time. Building a splendid new house on the most elevated part of the Isle of Sheppey helped to absorb and sooth my rather ragged thoughts at that time, and which at least became the ideal setting for my daughter's twenty-first birthday party.

The final pilotage
The structure of our lives however seemed fated, first my daughter decided to spread her wings, followed soon after by my son. The masterpiece of bricks and mortar set in half an acre became nothing more than a monument. My visits to the *Wellington* and other pursuits in London became more frequent and always unaccompanied. The annual trip to Estoril became more like every six months, little realizing it was all escapism with a steady deterioration in my health. Keeping pace was a decline in my vision – quietly having to use glasses to study a chart, with some difficulty in low visibility after prolonged peering. Eventually I was boarding ships with two pairs of spectacles, having to change quickly for checking the compass, radar screen or what-have-you. When the time came that the risks being taken were too great I saw the eye specialist, to whom it was admitted that some difficulty was experienced at the previous annual examination at Trinity House in reading the letters and colours. The bye-laws were quite clear on these matters and Trinity House being informed, an examination by their own appointed specialist was arranged before the necessary rigmarole regarding my licence was completed.

I piloted my last ship on 30 September 1967. It was a loaded 35,000 ton tanker flying the Greek flag inwards from the Nore to the Isle of Grain. In a sense it was a fitting final act of pilotage, which portrayed some of the turbulence, anxiety, politics and individualism ingrained in us. This was the little episode: As we stemmed the young ebb slowly approaching Garrison Point the steering broke down. In spite of the all too customary excited antics of the bridge personnel, an anchor was let go on to the bottom and a tug quickly made fast whilst the ship was still afloat. The steering fault was quickly fixed and in due course the ship was secured alongside the wharf. The greatly relieved captain was liberal with the whisky and unhesitatingly signed the pilotage note on which I had written the words: "From the Nore to the Isle of Grain via anchorage due to steering failure". The pilotage bill was sent to my solicitor, settling on my behalf a sum of £150 as 'extraordinary services' over and above the pilotage dues. Mercenary? No not really, just survival in a largely unsupported and precarious existence.

It came as a surprise to receive a kind of illuminated address on parchment, complete with colourful Trinity House crest and, with kind words from the Elder Brethren mentioning impaired eyesight. Kindly dated 30th January 1968 by the Secretary, it acknowledged the twentieth year of service as a Trinity House pilot in the London District.

A typical Scandinavian ship used in the pulpwood trade chartered by Bowaters Paper Mill at nearby Sittingbourne. She would be of pre-war vintage with a steam driven engine. Usually drawing about twenty feet they were not the best ships to handle bound inwards and loaded. There would always be a stern tide a little on the starboard quarter on the final approach to the Kingsferry Bridge. The average vessel on this trade would have a beam of between 40 and 44 feet, whilst the distance between the bridge buttresses was only 56 feet. In order to maintain good steerage, at least half speed was necessary, so that one can imagine how tense an operation it was – also how serious the odd accident's affect had on traffic communication.

Outward the ship would always be stemming the tide, this made for better steering but the danger lay with cross winds when, always flying light the ship would make leeway, thereby tending to approach the bridge opening crab-fashion.

81

11. Sierra Leone

There was little doubt in my mind regarding the insurance under which, should one of my faculties fail, the underwriters of the policy would pay a stipulated annual sum until I reached the age of sixty-five. So secure did I feel with my two policies that I contemplated withdrawing my entire contributions in the Pilots Benefit Fund. It was quite a shock therefore when a letter was received from the insurance company saying that my impaired eyesight was general degeneration due to advancing years and, under the terms of the policy accepted no responsibility! It was a great relief when my solicitors quickly settled that point. Firstly the Norwich Union offered a lump sum in settlement, which was declined; then they commenced regular quarterly payments under the terms of the two policies. With the small Trinity House pension that I had decided to accept, I thought my income would be adequate.

Of course it was all wishful thinking. Barely fifty-five, I soon discovered my store of vigour was sufficient to induce restlessness and a need for some worthwhile occupation. Not surprisingly, life with a 'has-been' became unbearable for my wife (we pilots tended to be big frogs in a small pool on the Isle of Sheppey) so, off she went to be with her sister in the West Country.

It was during the period leading up to this fateful juncture of my life that my two children, not content with 'flatting' in London, decided to leave England altogether. My daughter joined Pan American Airways, being based in Florida, whilst my son settled for Australasia. A smaller house had been built on adjoining land and our beautiful 'monument' sold.

It was little wonder therefore that early in 1968 I found myself in Harley Street, London, being subjected to a fairly rigourous medical examination by the Sierra Leone Selection Trust's doctor, with view to being appointed a plant security officer at their diamond mine. The advertisement had called for ex-service officers not below the rank of Lieutenant Commander, and aged between fifty and fifty-five. So, with a good supply of pills to keep my blood pressure under control and complete with the propulsive genetics within me I flew off – severing the umbilical cord to salt water.

Needless to say, at Freetown Airport memories came back to me of *Aubretia* and the convoy escort days of the war with the equatorial sweltering heat.

Having completed the routine immigration formalities we took off in the company's Heron aeroplane. The pilot, a German ex-mercenary, gave us a close-up birds eye view of the four hundred odd miles of African jungle to our destination. It was a remarkable experience.

The Yengama Mining Camp lay in what was probably a large shallow prehistoric crater, up to which the two thousand feet high rim, would have been a steady and long ascent through dense tropical-like rain forest, well watered by the four to six month heavy rain season, hence the myriads of mosquitoes. The term camp suggested to the mind tents and things. Not so; the mining staff and their families occupied lovely bungalows set in trees and dotted all around the eighteen hole golf course. Included in this park-like setting was the main administrative office block, the 'chop' store which stocked just about everything imaginable and a school for the mining staff children. There was a small well equipped hospital with qualified medical staff. But of the greatest service to all of the expatriates was The Club. One and all, including children and mine managers, would spend most of their leisure time cooling off in the pool or relaxing with cold drinks in the spacious club rooms. The evenings were particularly pleasant, when wives with their off duty husbands could meet their friends, play games or gossip. Those hours were most enjoyable. At my interview in London the golf course was mentioned and the selected odd numbered irons with the even woods (just enough extra weight for the plane) worked in very well with the course. There was a well run club with captain and committee, also a substantial list of tournaments to encourage play most of our free time.

I cannot remember with certainty what our number was, about twelve security officers I believe, including our chief whom we nicknamed 'Snudge' because he resembled that well known character in the television comedy "Bootsy & Snudge". Actually that was where the similarity ended, because prior to Sierra Leone he was a high ranking Scotland Yard man. We worked in three shifts, each officer being allocated two of the total six 'plants' comprising the mine. The layout can best be described by thinking of the palm of one's hand, the centre of the palm being residential and administration, leading from which the workshops, transport depot and along to the fingertips the six individual plants. In between the fingers and beyond the tips were dotted the areas of opencast mining, with an interlacing unsurfaced network of tortuous roads. Using German VW cars all fitted with VHF radio communication, each security officer responded to code calls from the plants. With the exception of one plant only, engaged crushing kimberlite rock for diamond extraction, the other plants were supplied with gravel from the opencast workings and, brought in by heavy ten tonne lorries.

Each plant had an engineer responsible for the production of the 'concentrate' (or heavy mineral). They were mostly expatriate personnel but included were a few black West African qualified engineers. Each of the shift engineers and the security officer would hold separate sets of keys for the double locking systems of the several theft-potential places in the plant. Additionally, each plant had its own vault. The engineer and security officer each possesed separate code sets of numbers necessary to operate the double locking access. Although the plants were enclosed in a perimeter of expanded metal fencing, carefully calculated illegal entry was a possibility. However, no sentries or extraordinary surveillance was considered necessary in addition to the very effective double locking systems.

The gravel on arriving at the plant was dumped in an area half the size of a football pitch. This was referred to as the 'mat', along which a mechanical endless scoop supplied a constant ribbon of gravel on to an inclined upwards moving belt, reaching the highest part of the plant. From here it commenced its complicated journey. First there was a large metal seive-like grating which was called the cyclone, then there was a cylinder also very huge which they called the trundle. Larger objects in the gravel at this stage were skilfully separated and diverted to be processed in a different manner. Water was introduced to the gravel in a large round tank, similar to a garden swimming pool. A constant circular motion of the mixture caused the

The mine manager's residence overlooking the golf course

heavy minerals to find their way towards the side of the 'Plan' as it was called. At regular and frequent intervals this concentrated heavier muck was extracted in an ingenious way by the opening and closing of a small door. This was one of the double-lock points of inspection used by the engineer, and referred to as the No 1 pan tap-off. From this point the heavy mineral went down to a similar second tank where the same process was continued and, where yet another similar tap-off point (No. 2 pan tap-off) was double locked. These inspections took place two or three times each shift so, with the two plants this alone contributed to being alert.

No doubt readers will like to know where the lovely diamonds come in. By the time the concentrate is leaving the No. 2 pan it is becoming smaller in quantity, but heavier in density, and finds its way with the flow of water to a third and final round pan. From this much smaller (re-con.) pan the circular motioned water is being constantly ejected, leaving the heavy mineral to settle and steadily build up on the bottom.

Once only each shift, in a reinforced section immediately beneath the re-con pan, a chute in the ceiling (not unlike the periscope control) is opened to allow the final concentrate to pour down into a portable container. Entry to this tap-off section is of course double locked and only two men in addition to the engineer and security officer allowed entry. This is a vital part of the operation because sometimes the actual diamonds are visible, and can spill on to the concrete floor. The lithe and sinewy Africans with a swift eye could pick a diamond with their toes or pop one in the mouth as quick as lightning. This was part of the job and if necessary we man-handled them on the spot. A portion of this section was a reinforced concrete vault, the door to which was opened by two different sets of number combinations – these numbers had to be remembered by the plant security officer and engineer separately. Each container of concentrate was lead-sealed with date and plant number before locking away in vault. The chute in the ceiling was doubled locked, the floor carefully hosed down with water which was drained away and returned into the plant system, before finally double locking this floodlit section.

The continuous processing of the gravel was frequently interrupted by a malfunction of the system, usually something to do with the pumping. But occasionally it would be sabotage, cleverly arranged to produce an exposed buildup of concentrate, which in turn would distract the engineer. Invariably incidents such as these were organized when the security officer was not at the plant and, these were the occasions when upon receipt of a VHF message (padlock call), our drivers would step on it and go like hell – until we arrive to supply the second pair of eyes and complete the double locking system. That crucial period was a suitable time for the illicit acquiring of diamonds.

This account of the mining would not be complete without some explanation of the final stages of the concentrate. Once each morning at around 8am a mobile armed guard with the senior security officer, would usually collect three containers from each plant and deliver them to a strongly built enclosure sited close to the administrative block. The building resembled a small prison, strict identification being carried out each time any person was given entry or exit. In rotation, each security officer would perform a whole week of duty at this separator house. In order to remove the diamonds from the mass of discoloured heavy mineral, a row of six machines called 'vaners', manipulated endless greased belts on to which there was a constant flow of water. The heavy mineral was steadily deposited from above on to this slightly sloping greased belt. Diamonds having perfectly flat facets would stick to the greased belt, whilst all non-precious mineral would be washed quickly off the belt. From that point the diamonds went through a thorough cleaning process to remove the countless years of earth discolouration. Then would follow sorting, disgarding and weighing of the stones, after which they were placed in large square tough paper envelopes before being locked away in the main vault under the scrutiny of the government inspector. Once again the vault would be double locked – the chief engineer completing the combinations.

At irregular and unannounced times, a helicopter would touch down inside the enclosure and with swift precision, under armed guard, collect the packaged diamonds and whisk them away to Freetown. At the time of which I write, close to a million pounds worth of uncut diamonds were mined each day.

After this interesting and rather pleasant daily routine had continued for a few months, the camp life style was interrupted when a section of the Sierra Leone Army staged a coup uncomfortably close to Yengama. It was short lived and things soon settled back to normal. Unfortunately, some months later a second coup took place, this time much closer to the camp. Management announced that those wishing to terminate their contracts would be flown home free. I joined those thoughtful for the safety of their skins and returned to the United Kingdom. It had all been a very, very interesting experience.

12. Australia

It was late summer of 1968 when I returned to the United Kingdom. But even a short break at Las Palmas did not dispel a growing feeling of despair as the plane flew northward – the future was beginning to worry me. Being on call at all times as a Trinity House Pilot was generally considered not the ideal way to live but neither was an aimless existence conducive to making a contented future. Almost as if it were an unpleasant dream, opening my front door to emptiness was the last straw.

Purchasing a fairly new and, sturdy little Morris 1000 car, I imagined that a trip to the Continent would in some way do me good. From Calais I drove to Ostende and made my way through the Belgium lowlands in to Germany. I remember enjoying the drive along the main roads, with only reduced autumn traffic to contend with. It was my first experience of the German autobahn. Crossing the Rhine I eventually reaching my objective in Dortmund. It helped to dispel some of the unpleasant thoughts of the years that lay ahead of me.

The beer-gardens and fraulines however were not the cure; soon I was making my way toward Luxemburg, to see for myself and discover how true were the romantic stories told by the air-pilot at Yengama. Regrettably, although the city of Luxemburg was fascinating, my lasting memories were only of the famous clocks with their intricate figure movements.

I arrived back in England with my mind made up – the only thing to do was a final plea for a marital reunion and, failing of that, book a passage out to Australia where my son was now settled.

An uneasy Christmas was spent with my married sister in the Midlands and, on 4th January 1969 I sailed from Southampton on the *Canberra*. As from that time, a certain measure of guilt feeling became my constant innermost thought, something which I fear will remain with me to the end.

One positive thing was how good it was to be back aboard ship, even if only as a passenger. I soon discovered the name of the *Canberra's* master – Captain E.G.H. Riddelsdell, RD, RNR, (Rtd) – and soon after 'making my number' was invited to his quarters, where we swapped acquaintances over our gin. I was pleased to accept his freedom of the bridge, a small token, but inwardly satisfying the recognition of the forty odd million tons of shipping I had handled as a pilot. He struck me as being a fine shipmaster, frequently circulating among the passengers with something to say to most of them. The private party on the captain's deck was a huge success, one never to forget! By the time the ship was off the West African coast, most people seemed to have formed their own little groups. Apart from the troop-ship during the war, this was my first experience as a passenger and, I found the life both interesting and stimulating.

Freedom of the Bridge

Commander T. G. Radford.

I should like you to consider yourself free to visit the Bridge whenever you wish to during your passage with us.

C. G. H. Riddell
CAPTAIN

There was no shortage of entertainment, including live shows, dancing every night, film theatre, much patronized swimming pools and, my favourite evening pastime – the casino. The scheduled ports of call were Cape Town, Durban, Fremantle, Adelaide, Melbourne and Sydney. The particular group with which I had become friendly were keen sight-seeing kind of people and, although I had been to Cape Town several times, it was not until then that the cable-car thrill to the top of Table Mountain was experienced.

The voyage was more like a cruise than a straight passage from A to B, our visit to a Melbourne night-club for example – I was not expecting to revive those kind of frolics! The first to leave our particular group was a builder and his wife, at Fremantle, where at Perth he hoped to set up his sign-board. They were fine people, he was so proud of his motorcar – even had it shipped out with much concern as to whether it would be there for his arrival. Saying goodbye to short-lived friendships was sad, so many of us were taking on the unknown with trepidation – I wonder how they fared.

I disembarked at Sydney on 3rd February 196; it was the hottest day, so they said, in memory. To me it seemed worse than the Persian Gulf. My English summer clothes were totally unsuitable, I remember those first few days of extreme discomfort very well. The third day I returned to the *Canberra* for drinks, thoroughly fed up with the heat and, rather disillusioned with the standard of accommodation available. Captain Riddelsdell told me there was still a vacant berth available should I wish to return with the ship to the U.K. When we shook hands he gave me until noon the following day for my answer if accepting.

It was that something in my nature I suppose – 'nil desperandum' and all that – that made me stick it out, but for several weeks I bitterly regretted not accepting the *Canberra* offer.

The amateur gamblers at the casino evening session. My white shirt and bow tie makes me look more like the croupier.

13. The Bosun's Locker

As time went on I realized that that the antipodean life style differed in many ways from the societies I had been accustomed to. The search for peace of mind and personal comfort, I discovered, was producing a kind of self denial of my former way of living. As I write this, living on a small island in the South Pacific, I confess to being more confused now about the business of living than ever.

Gradually I settled down, the bed-sitter being the most difficult thing to come to terms with; however, with an old 1956 Austin and two or three friends, I survived those first two or three months. The temperature simply had to come down a little and with some shopping for appropriate clothing, things started to improve somewhat.

The real break came when one of my friend's brother decided to give his job up in the city. After a satisfactory meeting with his employers the job became mine and, straight away commenced the stock-taking procedures. Little had I imagined that my searching for work would materialize into managing a nautical supplies establishment – which was precisely the job I had landed. It was called the **Bosun's Locker**, situated close to the northern end of the Sydney Harbour Bridge. It belonged to two partners, both keen yachtsmen, one being of the famous Halvorsen boat building family. I soon discovered that the 'Locker' was just another of their absorbing hobbies, also that it was a very expensive one judging by the quality and range of items for sale.

It would be no exaggeration to say the total number of different items for sale would be in the region of four figures, most of which could be described as objects of beauty, value and, craftsmanship. From memory, the extensive range included such eye-catching small ship items and gifts as: heavy based highball glasses, each cleverly inscribed with the coloured international code flags, storm warnings, rule of the road advice or flag signals with interpretations, and gaily designed place mats of historic maps, small ship rules or other useful nautical information; high quality items of scrimshaw in the form of bookends, rings, tie-pins, earrings and paper-weights. Of special attraction were the hand-made ship model kit-sets, a selection of which were expertly made up and were the subject of constant intensely interested scrutiny. The selection of kit-sets were extensive, from the famous Swedish *Vasa* to the comparatively modern *Cutty*

Sark. Many famous American vessels of the days of sail were repre-sented among the kits, including the first of America's Cup race winners, the schooner yacht *America*. This side of the business also included almost every kind of cannon used in history's wars, from the privateer one-pounder to the breach-loader Whitworth cannon used in the American Civil War. Both the ships and cannons were authentic and perfect in detail, right down to the little blocks, cleats, belaying-pins, anchors, chains, rope, rigging and even the sliding wooden tops to the companionways.

There were lamps galore, brass and copper, some regulation size and most popular for placing outside ones front door. Like most of the other items these lamps were expensive, especially the hanging cabin style. Some of the shades were of attractive fabric or heavy parchment depicting old maps of different parts of the world, alto-gether a gleaming sight. Here and there were brass and chrome clocks and barometers, dozens of them – big and small and, quite suitable for all classes of shipping.

An interesting side of the business was a fine selection of nautical prints, mostly by well known artists like M. Dawson. Many of the more rare and costly were framed, giving the establishment a yet more scintillating appearance – a kind of nautical Aladdin's cave. My favourite was the clipper *Thermopylae* by Montague Dawson (approx. 4' x 3') leaving Foochow harbour. In time my knowledge of prints and lithographs developed and it became apparent that the acquisition of certain items was to the credit of the astute partnership. To own a line drawing of an early sailing vessel, published by one Hugh Evelyn of London (of which we held a few), would be a joy today.

This account of the Locker would not be complete without mentioning the several replica figureheads always in stock. With an overall length of about four feet, space was somehow found on the wall or in a corner for these flamboyant, but lifelike figures. Very few people failed to gaze at the "Mystic Belle", with her brown wavy hair, red dress with white ruffles and lovely large breasts bursting her low cut bodice. By now the reader will no doubt agree that the Bosun's Locker was an unusual place of work – to say the least. Fortunately the partners allowed me to run this fascinating establishment on a fairly free rein. Most of the stock was supplied from overseas, America, Germany, Holland, England and Italy. Cash was sent abroad in the form of drafts arranged at the local bank; this was a lengthy business, with frequent holdups for customs clearance. Being a master mari-ner, the application we made for the agency, to stock and sell Royal

Australian and British Admiralty charts, was granted, so, with the Sailing Directions and regular supplies of corrections, the business grew.

It was either advancing years, or the daily tedious rail journey to the home I had built half way up the Blue Mountains, that eventually caused some stress and discomfort; regular chest pains developed as I rushed to catch my evening train home. On one such day after a hold-up in the traffic, the run up the Central Station steps became too much exertion and, I barely made the last carriage sweating heavily with severe chest pain. After arriving at my little railway station, Springwood, the doctor very quickly had me on the road to hospital by ambulance, where I remained for four weeks.

The Bosun's Locker kept me in touch with the water, mostly yachties of course, but the odd professional of both services came my way. It was good to glean the tit-bits of information from time to time.

The *Melbourne/Evans* tragedy in 1970 was a very particular subject of conversation. The salient points of that catastrophe are still clear in my mind – it was a night exercise apparently with darkened ships and no steaming lights. The Australian carrier *Melbourne* having the flag, with the United States destroyer *Evans* part of the exercise fleet. I suppose there most have been some kind of official enquiry but, from the scraps of news available, it seemed the officer of the watch in the *Evans* had had only a short period of sea experience. It was also alleged the flag officer aboard the *Melbourne*, together with the captain were below, both having left night orders to be called if necessary. It seems that when collision was imminent, the avoiding action caused the *Evans* to be cut through amidships by the *Melbourne*, causing the loss of seventy-two lives.

It is easy to become an armchair critic of course but difficult to understand a later calamity when a brand new Australian naval vessel, on a shake-down trial, hit rocks and ripped her bottom open. More recently we read about the HMAS *Wollongong* running aground. In this instance it seems there was a court martial.

Maritime history during these last few decades is strewn with evidence of technological (sic.) 'progress' not always being accompanied by a more practical application, for example the *Truculent* affair or even the *Amoco Cadiz*. In all the years I was at sea, there was never a sighting of the coastline at or near Ushant, the N.W. point of France where the *Amoco Cadiz* struck with such catastrophic results. The very infrequent occasions when Ushant Light was sighted would have been the rare patches of exceptionally fine weather in that particular area. For this reason ships gave the point a very wide berth – fifty miles would not be uncommon. With the adoption of radar there appeared a tendency to adopt a sense of security and the distance off these salient points became less. Under these circumstances therefore, the 'electronic eye', or any other piece of vital electronically operated part of the ship, can tend towards additional hazard.

Already, I was discovering that leisure and the time devoted to it down under, had a much greater emphasis than back home in England. Weekends and public holidays stretched ahead like sign-posts, and were looked forward to as a calculated and determined experience of a particular pleasure. Everybody seemed hell-bent on savouring to the full the unequalled beauty and fascination of their fabulous continent. Winmalee, the spot we had picked near Springwood, thirteen hundred feet up in the Blue Mountains, was a wonderful site on virgin gum studded land on which our house was built. The famous rosellas, each a splash of red green and yellow, were birds of constant attraction, as were the less attractive kookaburra but not lacking in vociferousness. These, like many other creatures such as the koala bear, goanna and bell bird were all harmlessly fascinating, making the Australian bush unequalled for its beauty. Along with their creamy white beaches and these exotic animals, not to mention the unspoiled natural beauty, it seemed strange that this vast country of spectacular landscapes had not acquired a much bigger population.

Our little section in the gum trees at Winmalee was only a stone's throw from the Hawksbury road. Eastward it descends, winding its way down from the Blue Mountains. Here and there through openings in the trees were flashes of the Hawksbury River well below, curving and sweeping its way to the sea. On reaching the lowland the gum trees noticeably thin out giving way to well tended large market gardens, orange groves or horse ranches. The houses, sparsely dotted with their deep verandas, always gave me the impression of tranquillity. Tourists and possibly city dwellers would tend to make for Katumba, at the summit of the Blue Mountains, there to marvel at the spectacular Three Sisters, or other lookout spots. We however preferred the lower reaches. It was there we would find the dried-up water courses in which we loved to fossick for the multi-coloured hard stone and, always the hope of finding a small fragment of gold. The five dollar miners licence was certainly cheap for the amount of pleasure it provided.

Not even this brief description of this part of New South Wales would be adequate without a word or two about Mr Fish and Mr Chips. These, believe it or not, were the two trains which left the Blue Mountains each weekday morning. The Fish, so called since the inaugural days of the railway when the engine driver's name happened to be Fish arrived at Sydney Central at about 8am. The Chips, also named after an earlier engine driver, was scheduled to arrive about a half hour later in the City.

I always caught the 'chips', never tiring of the daily train journey winding and snaking its way along the sides of the Blue Mountains, with their breathtaking views along the steep mountain sides – a never to be forgotten experience.

Although the motive seemed valid at the time, in retrospect it must be admitted that the reasons my partner and I decided to cross the Tasman are now somewhat inexplicable but such is the business of living.

14. New Zealand

Once before, during 1967, my daughter and I had visited this remote part of the Commonwealth, we were performing a kind of whirlwind tour of the antipodes hoping to find traces of my son, from whom no word had been received for eighteen months.

I remember my first impressions of Auckland and country round about very clearly, resembling the English West Country of pre-war days. Fiercely the people protected their independence – "There is no tipping here" said the chap who helped us with our luggage at the air-port.

Reunited with my son Peter

Four years later, with Australia under my belt, stepping ashore at Auckland from the Greek owned *Australis* did not produce any evidence of much change. The twelve year old boy had flown over ahead with our one year old dog, so it was left to me to attend to the pile of luggage, the sea-sickened prostrate mother having been taken by ambulance to hospital. Eventually the car was unloaded and all formalities completed. A miraculous change in my partner's health had earned her speedy discharge.

Cambridge, the small Waikato town reminded us of England, so we decided to look no further and we purchased an old brick built house very much in need of attention. For the first eight months I worked very hard, tackling jobs well outside my normal range of activity, but with the help of a builder all the work was finally completed. I was very proud of my efforts in connection with No. 23 Grey Street, feeling sure that Mr Edwards the Welsh builder would also have been pleased to see the house built fifty-two years previously looking so smart and up-to-date.

Spread across a winding section of the Waikato River, Cambridge was noted for its great variety of trees, boasting also a lake and village green style reserve right in the middle of the little town.

Surrounded by well grown trees this expanse of grass was the local cricket ground, all contributing to the English impression we originally formed.

Toward the end of the year with summer having arrived we started to explore the North Island's wonderful sights. Our home was an excellent point of departure, with places of interest radiating in several directions. These trips were reserved for the week-ends and we looked forward to them with great pleasure. At the time of which I write the car was fairly new, having brought it with us from Australia, so distances were of little consequence. Traffic congestion was unknown and it was not uncommon to drive for half an hour without seeing another vehicle.

Unlike Australia, New Zealand resembles more the U.K., more compact with distances far less, thus allowing return journeys to places of interest within one day. (Without the motor-car of course the reverse would apply, public transport having not kept pace with the march of time.)

The more distant places like Doubtless Bay and Mangonui in the far north however could well be completed with only one night away

No.23 Grey Street - Cambridge

Restored to its former glory as the typical colonial middle class residence, this was the result of our first year's hard work. Built by Edwards in the early twenties it was unique for that area being constructed in 'cavity brick' method. Determined to cling to his Welsh heritage the house was called Rhyl, but unfortunately this was not known until well after the old unfaced red bricks had received at least three coats of white paint. By this time we had christened the house Sternend after the brass stern light (seen beside the front door) which we had brought with us from Australia, along with our dear dog Tim standing in the foreground.

from home. Such a place was Whangaroa near the N.E. tip of North Island – very much a part of the country's history. (In 1809 the sailing vessel *Boyd*, whilst anchored in the natural harbour loading kauri spars, was attacked by the local Maori tribesman. Only a handful of the seventy souls on board survived the massacre, one a very small young child called Betsy Broughton, of whom much more could be written. She survived to rear seventeen children in Australia and lived to a ripe old age.)

Rightfully, the New Zealanders are proud of their short history, respecting the well preserved things like the old stone house at Keri Keri and the treaty house at Waitangi as the tangible evidence. Relics of the whaling industry are dotted along the eastern coastline, together and the gold recovery industry of the Coromandel Peninsula is still very much alive – as evidenced by local environmentalists who wish to preserve the unspoiled beauty of this fascinating peninsula.

Eventually No. 23 Grey Street was restored to its original well-found state, plus some up-dating, so my attention moved to some gainful occupation. Cambridge will be remembered for my initiation into the farming world by joining Dalgety, the stock and land agents. Through them I learned the technique and language of the land agent, from the sale and purchase of houses and sections of land, through to a fair knowledge concerning bales to the acre or livestock thereto on the very productive Waikato soil.

It seems my professional calling was still strong in me when during January 1975 I signed a contract with Waipipi Iron Sands Limited in connection with the duties of mooring master for ship loading operations. This of course was in addition to the real estate interests and some thought this second string was too much for a person in their sixties – which was proved correct in due course. The parent company was American, known as the Marcona Corporation. Cargo was loaded at an off-shore single point mooring, the iron sand being mixed with water to form a slurry and then pumped through a submarine pipeline

There were one or two unusual aspects of the overall operation. Maritime aspects were under the jurisdiction of the Wanganui Harbour Board (some twenty miles eastward along the coast) whose harbour master was kept fully informed. Waipipi Iron Sands Limited was concerned with overall administration, having an American manager and Marcona itself participating the bills of lading and all movements. The Japanese manned ships of some fifty to seventy-five thousand tonnes were chartered, with arrival notices being sent in sufficient time for me to secure a flight from Hamilton Airport to Wanganui. From there a company car would take me to hotel accommodation at the small country town of Waveley. The work itself was shared with the resident senior pilot/loading master, boarding and unshipping of the vessels being carried out solely by means of helicopter.

It was this off-shore aspect of the operation which, in my opinion, completely changed the concept of the normal ship's business of arriving at a port, loading a cargo, then sailing away on its business venture. Excepting cases of emergency, the pilot was the only person making contact with the vessel's presence in New Zealand territorial waters (with the exception of the helicopter pilot when parked on board awaiting the boarding of the departing pilot/loading-master). It followed therefore that all the formalities normally carried out by customs officials, shipping agents, health and maritime port authorities, shore cargo personnel, together with people like stores representatives, all essential to a ship's visit, became the concern to varying degree of the pilot mooring-master.

These important aspects of the vessel's presence within New Zealand waters were, in my opinion, a separate concern and should have been the responsibility of a qualified shipping agent appointed by the management, thus leaving the professional ship-handler to attend to the safety and efficiency of the vessel's presence at the potentially precarious single point mooring (with the ship secured by means of two fifteen-inch polypropylene ropes), a little more than one mile off an exposed coastline.

With my daughter at Titirangi 1979

A concluding observation concerning the iron sand offshore operation deals with the helicopter method of shipping and unshipping. Particularly at night during adverse weather conditions with wind approaching gale force, I consider the ship-pilot's departure operation extremely hazardous and should be with that person's sole discretion.

The year 1976 came bringing big changes; we sold our house and moved away North to Waiheke Island, a beautiful forty-odd square mile island set twelve miles down the Hauraki Gulf from Auckland. At a spot where all shipping using the port of Auckland was visible, yet another house was built. It was a superb position with views across the Gulf stretching from the Coromandel coast to the east, through the distant Barrier Islands across to the Whangapararoa Penninisula on the mainland. After resigning my contract with the Waipipi Iron Sand – it called for a younger person really – there still remained the search for some gainful and suitable employment.

It would be fair to say that people of my background tended to scoff at ordinary office workers, in my case driving a desk job would have been out of the question. So it was with very much mixed feelings that I commenced working for one of the large primary products exporters. Theirs was a large office overlooking Auckland Harbour (I used to think it was some kind of retribution for past sins) and had it not been for having to be totally absorbed in my duties, I think much of the time would have been pleasantly spent gazing down at all the harbour movements. I soon fitted in to this army of pen-pushers; we were about two hundred men and women occupying the top floor of this large building at the wharf edge. A casual visitor seeing this large group of people bent over their desks could well be surprised to learn that the paper-work was all to do with the processing of animals, cheese and butter. For five days a week it was a clockwork life, rising early each morning and through the repetitive paper world of the eight hour day – then back home with the tide-like surge of traffic.

Then came my sixty-fifth birthday, and in accordance with the rules I became a 'beneficiary' so, with my Trinity House pension (happily increased about this time) together with the tiny war pension, I felt financially secure for the first time in my life. I decided to retire completely from any form of gainful activity.

Living then at one end of the Waitakere Range, within walking distance of the spectacular scenic reserve, gave little excuse for not enjoying a pleasant and peaceful retirement. The days were taken up pottering around my quarter acre or in the little basement workshop.

The neighbours were good and kind with a regular wave from the children as they passed my frontage all clean and spruced for their day at school. Every Tuesday evening was club night and this regular meeting with particular friends was eagerly anticipated. In my experience there is no match for the warmth and pleasant satisfaction of being among fellow officers of one's own time. (Later I was pleased and honoured to become a life member of the Auckland Officers' Club.)

In this relaxed state of generally doing things when and how I pleased, it was no hardship for me to drive each Sunday morning to Auckland, there to attend either the Anglican Cathedral or the tiny kauri built St.Stephens. The people were very friendly and our cross black spaniel, Tim, never to be left behind – became a great favourite at the after-service churchyard romp. I found myself on the Dean's list within a short time, and, after a little instruction joined a roster of Cathedral Guides. Attending the tea-parties given by the Dean's wife was most interesting – they were a wonderful couple, reminding me of peace-time naval life.

After years of legal wrangling my marriage was dissolved in June 1982, and a few months later I remarried. The Titirangi property was sold and my wife's place at Mission Bay was also disposed of. This would have been the appropriate moment to shake the dust of New Zealand off our shoes and either return to Australia or the United Kingdom. People sometimes however do things which they later realized to be a mistake – that being exactly what happened when we decided to return to a permanent residence here on Waiheke Island.

Aotearoa! Why consider leaving such a beautiful place in the South Pacific would be a fair question? Why indeed. In honesty it must be said the reason was complex and cannot be explained simply. Perhaps the reader will be able to draw their conclusions after reading the remaining events which extend into the year 1987.

15. An Old Sailor

In 1980 I received a letter from Desmond Wettern (Lieutenant RNR) in England. Desmond happens to be the honorary secretary of the Royal Naval Reserve Officers' (London) Club, but is better known for his articles dealing with the Royal Navy, which are published in the *Daily Telegraph* and other outlets with a nautical flavour. The letter was about the late master mariner, my friend Captain Stephen Polkinghorn, DSC. Giving me Stephen's address he wanted me to pay him a visit, and obtain a brief summary of his life and exploits.

Now in his ninities, he lived alone in a small unit, managing to walk with his stick to a nearby shop for the odd requirement. His needs were few and both his daughters paid regular visits. The Meals-on-Wheels provided the essential one good meal per day. He was never idle, spending much of his time at his desk typing letters to a host of people; his eldest son, the headmaster of a school in the U.K., old shipmates including his last chief officer (Lewis), then living out his life in Suva. He was a great reader and introduced me to some of the best books with a slant of the sea that I have ever read.

Captain Stephen Polkinghorn, D.S.C. This photograph was taken during March 1984 at the Ranfurly Veterans Home, where he occupied a private room with his books, pictures, radio and much used little typewriter

Stephen was supposed to have run away to sea at a very early age, but it does seem he commenced an apprenticeship about the turn of the century in the full rigged ship *Cromdale*, a wool clipper of some 2000 tons running to Australia. Considering the rigours of that life with Cape Horn to boot, something from those days must have brought about his strength of mind and body. He kept a strict account of receipts and expenditure which, obviously was a carry-on from his former days of dealing with disbursement and portage bills.

For a time during the first world war, Stephen Polkinghorn served as chief officer of a troop ship called *Wai-Shing*, running between India and the Persian Gulf. It was about this time he decided to join the Royal Naval Reserve. Between the first and second world wars Stephen first served with Butterfield & Swire (old established shipowners on the Eastern and Pacific trade), and then became a pilot on the Pei-Ho river in China.

With the outbreak of the 1939-45 War, Lieutenant Polkinghorn was appointed in command of a river gunboat and earned his niche in history. Best described by the author Richard Story in his book *Japan and the decline of the West in Asia 1894-1943*, in which the opening paragraph goes something like this:-

It was four o'clock in the morning of the 8th December 1941, when moored off the Bund at Shanghai lay the sole surviving representative of British Naval Power, the Yangstze gunboat H.M.S. *Peterel* (the mis-spelling of the sea bird Petrel was attributable to an Admiralty office worker prior to commissioning, which it was decided never to correct). Her commanding officer Lieutenant Stephen Polkinghorn RNR was fifty-seven years of age. Within a few hundred yards of *Peterel* were three Japanese warships.' Upon hearing that the International Settlement was being taken over by Japanese forces, Lieut. Polkinghorn sent all hands to action stations and set about the destruction of his cyphers and confidential books. Within ten minutes the chief of staff of the Japanese Commander-in-Chief came on board demanding the immediate surrender of H.M.S. *Peterel*. Lieut. Polkinghorn is alleged to have refused in no uncertain terms, ordering the emissary off his ship. Within minutes the Japanese opened fire with gun and machine-gun fire from all sides. Soon *Peterel* was ablaze fore & aft and the Commander ordered demolition charges to be fired and abandon-ship.

The gallant conduct of Lieutenant Polkinghorn – says the Admiralty report – in defying the Japanese who called on him to surrender his ship, attracted a great deal of attention and much favourable comment in China itself. The survivors, all of whom were wounded, spent the remainder of the war in Woosung (China) and later in Japan as prisoners of war. (Little did old Polkie know that he had been awarded the DSC) At the end of hostilities and his release, he returned to sea commanding ships owned by Burns Philp, in his best known Pacific. He retired in 1960.

At 0400hrs on 29th December 1985, my old friend Stephen Polkinghorn passed away at the Ranfurly War Veterans Home, where he had been in good hands for a couple of years. He tried desperately hard to last out for his one hundredth birthday message from the Queen, and the strength in his grip on my wrist the day before he went made me think he would pull through, but he had to settle for ninety-nine. Two days later on the 31st December 1985 I was privileged to help carry him on the final voyage.

16. Finalé

My completion of half a century in the workforce was no mean accomplishment. It encompassed a world wide venue with continuous wartime active service covering six years. Therefore it is little wonder that my range of targets for comment tend to be wide. Sometimes I discover myself confusing issues, which are quickly pounced upon by those at whom the arrows are directed. Taking upon myself this watch-dog kind of attitude has brought in its train both reward and incensement, but it has also helped me (now in my seventies) to stay reasonably alert and aware of what goes on around us.

Many years ago I read about an obscure Welsh parson of the 17th century whom was alleged to have said, "You will never enjoy the world aright till the sea floweth in your veins, till you are clothed with the heavens and crowned with the stars". The words perhaps explain why, as the north-east winter gale blows with driving rain at this very moment, in secure warmth at my desk my thoughts will stray to the discomfort and dangers aboard ship and offer up a word or two of thanks.

Waiheke Island for myself has been a kind of therapy, both for health, mind and interest. Forty years after escorting the battleship *Valiant* along with a couple of Polish ships filled with miscellaneous servicemen down the east coast of Africa, I discovered that our electrician here was taking passage in one of the Polish vessels – then a Royal Naval petty officer. From him I gathered his ship was the *Kosciuszki* (named after a Polish war hero) and that his neighbour was a Polish free fighter with the R.A.F. also taking passage in that convoy.

There are not many tar-sealed roads here on the Island, and fewer still favoured by the elderly people for easy walking. This house is on a level stretch with the little shopping area called Oneroa and it was fairly regularly that I used to see a man of my age passing by. After one or two morning greetings we engaged in conversation, his name was Wadsley and we soon discovered we had mutual acquaintances from the war days. The first discovery being one Captain Ouvry, RN, who was his mentor during the days they were engaged in the selfless and dangerous task of mine recovery. Within a short time our talks became almost a daily occurrence. We swapped yarns and found that quite often we knew the same people. Outstanding among these

From J. Ashe Lincoln, Q.C.

Tel. 01-353 7202
01-353 3506

9 Kings Bench Walk,
Temple,
London, EC4Y 7DX

5th September, 1985

Captain T.G. Radford, RN, FNI,
2A Mako Street,
Oneroa,
Waiheke Island,
New Zealand.

Dear Captain Radford,

I was delighted to receive from Desmond Wettern the letter which you sent him on the 2nd July. I was particularly pleased to have news of dear old Wadsley for whom I always had the highest regard and admiration. I hope you will pass on to him, my warmest good wishes and regards and tell him that I have the livliest recollection of that bleak day we spent together, recovering the first type G mine on the hills of Dumbarton. It was an historic moment from the point of view of the war effort. I am glad to hear that he is still in good health and full of activity.

I was also particularly interested to know that you actually sighted the U Boat which laid the Falmouth field, because as I think you will appreciate from my own account, it was only a guess on my part that those nine mines had been laid by a U Boat.

I am glad to say that Jack Pope comes yachting with me quite frequently, and we have many opportunities of exchanging memories of old times.

Thank you for your letter and with kindest regards.

Yours sincerely,

F. Ashe Lincoln

(Capt. RNVR).

mutually known was Captain Ashe Lincoln QC, RNVR, now our President of the Royal Naval Reserve Officers' (London) Club.

Here I must refer the reader back to my time on *East Moyra* (page 34). Subsequent to my U-Boat periscope sighting between Falmouth and Newlyn, the German minefield in that area which was submarine laid, became Ashe Lincoln's concern. But it was in Scotland on the hills of Dumbarton that Lieutenant Wadsley, RNVR, and Ashe Lincoln spent tense hours recovering the first type G mine, for which,with other extremely dangerous feats, they were highly decorated. I am happy to say 'Wads' and I now remain good friends, we discuss international events and both agree on how the world SHOULD be run!

And so finally, as I turn at my desk to reach for a book or some notes, I glance up at the higgledy-piggledy display of memorabilia. My whole life is there on the wall, from the indentures signed in 1929 to photographs of ships and shipmates, along with the parchments of Naval Commission, Competency, Freedom of the City of London, to the surrender of licence to Trinity House. It tells its own story of course, but it is good for my ego. A reply recently from the New Zealand Ministry of Transport concerning my offer of assessor services, was politely declined on account of my age – they are right, it is time to write FINISH.

Anzac Day